"Jordan's delightful *Day-Votions for Grandmothers* touched my heart as a grandmother of sixteen and brought many smiles of recognition. This sweet collection of 'grandma' stories will warm your spirit. I especially enjoyed the story about Beanie Babies—since I have four such 'babies' of my own!"

—Karen O'Connor, speaker and author of
Bein' A Grandparent Ain't For Wimps

"Rebecca's book is filled with sage wisdom, enlightening advice, and delightful stories. As a fairly new grandma, I'm eager to be encouraged by reading it often. You will be too."

—Kathy Collard Miller, speaker and author of *Why Do I Put So Much Pressure on Myself and Others?*

"Whether you're a Mimi, Nana, or Grams, this book is a must-read for grandmothers of all ages. Grab a cup of coffee or tea, sit down in your favorite chair, and take a moment to refresh your life with a Day-Votion each morning. Jordan's book is full of heartwarming stories all grandmothers will love."

—Edna Ellison, PhD, Christian mentoring guru
(www.ednaellison.com) and author of *A Passion for Purpose: 365 Devotions for Missional Living*

DAY-VOTIONS™
for grand mothers

*Heart to Heart
Encouragement*

Rebecca Barlow Jordan

ZONDERVAN.com/
AUTHOR**TRACKER**
follow your favorite authors

ZONDERVAN

Day-votions™ for Grandmothers
Copyright © 2010 by Rebecca Barlow Jordan

This title is also available as a Zondervan ebook.
Visit www.zondervan.com/ebooks.

This title is also available in a Zondervan audio edition.
Visit www.zondervan.fm.

Requests for information should be addressed to:

Zondervan, *Grand Rapids, Michigan 49530*

Library of Congress Cataloging-in-Publication Data

Jordan, Rebecca.
    Day-votions for grandmothers : heart-to-heart encouragement /
Rebecca Barlow Jordan.
        p.   cm.
    ISBN 978-0-310-32205-4 (hardcover, jacketed)
    1. Grandmothers — Prayers and devotions I. Title.
BV4847.J68 — 2009
242'.645 — dc22   2009040172

All Scripture quotations, unless otherwise indicated, are taken from the Holy Bible,
Today's New International Version™, *TNIV*®. Copyright © 2001, 2005 by Biblica,
Inc.™ Used by permission of Zondervan. All rights reserved worldwide.

Any Internet addresses (websites, blogs, etc.) and telephone numbers printed in
this book are offered as a resource. They are not intended in any way to be or imply
an endorsement by Zondervan, nor does Zondervan vouch for the content of these
sites and numbers for the life of this book.

Interior design: Michelle Espinoza

Printed in the United States of America

10 11 12 13 14 15 /DCI/ 20 19 18 17 16 15 14 13 12 11 10 9 8 7 6 5 4 3 2 1

To Haley, Jordan, Lauren, and Caden —
my very special grandchildren

contents

special thanks

In writing a book of encouragement for others, I must thank those who have encouraged me in the process. So many have had a part.

I'm so thankful for a great editor like Sue Brower who has been like a cheerleader — patiently encouraging, listening, answering questions, and believing in my writing. Her enthusiasm about this project from day one has filled me with an even greater passion to write my heart. You're the best, Sue! Thanks also to freelance editor Lori VandenBosch for her editing and encouraging comments, and to Verlyn Verbrugge for his editing skills. Thanks to marketing director Karwyn Bursma and her extremely talented team for their beautiful work on the book's cover and their creativity in marketing.

I appreciate Joyce Ondersma and Jackie Aldridge in author relations and the wonderful Zondervan sales team. And to the entire Zondervan staff, including support staff, for your willingness to publish this project. How can I say thank you enough for all you do? This book would not be possible without all of you at Zondervan.

A special thanks to Steve Laube, for his integrity and diligence as my agent and friend. His invaluable background and knowledge of the writing business have given superb direction to my writing. I so appreciate his encouragement and patience, his belief in my gifts, and his ability to find a home for my writing dreams so quickly. Thank you, Steve, for your enthusiasm for this new Day-votions series.

Thanks to my friend Karen-Atkins Milton, who gave generously of her time to look over many of these day-votions and offer another woman's perspective. To those who prayed for me throughout the writing of this book: my precious daughters and sons-in-law, Valerie, Jennifer, Shawn, and Craig, who also allowed me to share their stories; other family members, friends, church members, and my Bible study class; and the women of my personal, prayer support team: Priscilla Adams, Mary Griffin, Ruth Inman, Sharon Hogan, and Kim Coffman — your prayers and encouragement made such a difference. Thanks also to those moms, grand-moms, friends, and readers who shared transparent examples and stories from their lives or their grandmothers' in this book, which will no doubt encourage many in their walk with the Lord.

I also appreciate Warner Press for allowing me to use some bulletin and greeting card copy I wrote for them.

There is no way to adequately thank my precious husband for his prayers, support, and encouragement. Larry not only blessed me by offering his thorough editing skills and great communication abilities in reading through every day-votion. He also gave up his own comfort and rare personal time, taking over many of my everyday tasks to do whatever was necessary to help me complete this manuscript. With his love, integrity, and unselfishness he has influenced this writing more than anyone else, so that together, we could be a team in ministry. I could not write without his loving support. I love you, Larry! You are one of God's greatest blessings to me!

And to my precious heavenly Father and Lord Jesus, there will never be enough words to adequately praise you for who you are. Nor could I ever count the times you have continually blessed me in ways I could never deserve. For every time I cry, "I can't!" you always answer, "But I can!" You, Lord, are the passion of my heart. You are the One who encourages me daily, who satisfies my soul hunger, and who fills me with purpose. Thank you for allowing me the joy of writing about you and the privilege of sharing encouragement with others.

encouragement for grandmothers

"Grandmother" opens up a new world of change, challenge, and celebration in a woman's life. Grandmoms come in all shapes and sizes, but God stamps "original" on each of our lives. Our needs — and ages — vary. Whether we're young "Nanas," "boomer-grams," or "great-grams," we all crave understanding and companionship — other grandmoms, friends, and family members who will share our load and celebrate our joys.

And though we are unique individuals, every grandmother needs — and wants — encouragement and deeper, more meaningful relationships with her grandchildren, family, God, and others. Every grandmother longs to leave a legacy that will pass on from one generation to the next.

For years I've tried to write devotions that would encourage readers to connect on a deeper, more intimate level with God and others: to "love the Lord your God with all your heart and with all your soul and with all your strength and with all your mind" and to "love your neighbor as yourself" (Luke 10:27).

But sometimes "life" happens, and we grandmothers forget how to do that. We realize that love hurts and relationships take work. Growing older can zap our energy, change our perspective, and challenge our stability. Yet the longing to make a difference in the ones we love lingers, like the fragrance in a home when a sweet candle's flame has been extinguished.

In this new series of Day-votions™, I've tried to say to you as grandmothers, "You are not alone." None of us is. Our very existence depends on strong relationships. In bite-sized, *day-votions* for everyday living, I've written some nuggets of spiritual encouragement that I hope will help you strengthen your relationship with God, with your grandchildren and other family members, and with others. I pray these stories, insights, and biblical truths will direct you to the only One who can meet all of your needs. As you draw close to Jesus, I believe he will connect the dots to more meaningful relationships with others as well.

Whether you're struggling with aging, inadequacy, or fears, or celebrating with new beginnings, smiles, and tears, you are not alone. Other women have — and are — walking the same path as you. It doesn't matter if you're a single grandmother, married, middle-aged, or a senior, God is by your side, applauding your work, extending fresh hope, and drawing you close to himself so he can whisper, "You *are* making a difference. I'm here to help you, and I will take care of you. I love you. I always will."

Through these pages, I hope you'll laugh a little and maybe cry a little, but more than anything, my heart's desire is that you will be encouraged to keep on loving, laughing, serving, and sharing — and that you will gain a new sense of joy and purpose as you celebrate this beautiful God-ordained role of being a grandmother.

"May our Lord Jesus himself and God our Father, who loved us and by his grace gave us eternal encouragement and good hope, encourage your hearts and strengthen you in every good deed and word" (2 Thessalonians 2:16 – 17).

Rebecca

Grandmother Is a Name
Called Love

The kids may call her "Nana,"
"Gram," or even "Meems."
Her role is always changing—
That's the way it seems.
But one thing always stays the same:
Grandmother is a name called love.
She may dream of yesterday
and sigh in resignation;
or she may try to reinvent
her life and occupation.
But one thing always stays the same:
Grandmother is a name called love.

-RBJ

mothers forever

Give thanks to the Lord, for he is good; his love endures forever.
Psalm 118:1

Seven years passed, and still no change for my daughter. How many "tests" had she taken? And how many times had false hopes been raised? Too many to count. Lately, it seemed like all of her girlfriends had tummies growing with expectation of their first little ones, some even their second. Was it her imagination, or did their conversations sometimes fall to a hush when Jen approached them? Were they protecting her? When would her turn come?

She had begun medical testing, receiving fairly normal reports for both of them. That made it almost even harder. Because of the way Jen loved to surprise people, she hadn't told many, including us, that she was even trying to get pregnant.

Jen's doctor had performed the final test to see if she had blocked tubes. Her doctor discovered that one tube was indeed partially blocked, and considering her futile attempts to become pregnant, he suggested she see a "specialist" about a hundred fifty miles away.

Jen and Craig had sought prayer at their church from one of the elders. He prayed over them, asking God for a miracle to happen. In the meantime they had decided to go ahead and set the appointment for a specialist. Friends and family began praying.

The night before her specialist appointment, Jen called us about bedtime. She wanted us to pray for them and especially for God's will to be done. We thought it a little strange she would call so late, but given the circumstances, we agreed it was not too unusual. Five minutes later, the doorbell rang, and from the other room I heard my husband open the door and then a loud exclamation: "What in the world?" A burst of loud laughter followed.

I emerged from the bedroom and found my daughter and son-in-law standing in our living room. They lived four hours away. *How did you ...? But you just called!*

Seeing my obvious confusion, Jen explained, "We called from your driveway." It wasn't until that moment that I finally focused on the cause of the earlier laughter. Both Jen and Craig wore hand-painted T-shirts. Written on one were the words, "We've got a BUN in the oven." The other one read, "Are you ready to be called 'Me-Ma' and 'Pe-Po'"? (We had previously joked about such titles. Thankfully, the names didn't stick.)

Only four days earlier Jen had taken a home pregnancy test and discovered God had miraculously answered her prayers — just days before the scheduled specialist appointment. And in a matter of seconds, my life had changed too.

Once you're a mother, you're a mother forever.

It really doesn't matter what age or stage a mother is at. Once you're a mother, you're a mother forever. God places within each mom the need to nurture her little ones — always guiding, always loving, always giving and prodding them in the right direction with gentle reminders: "Be careful," "Dress warm," "Eat healthy." And just when you think the nest has emptied and mothering can take a vacation, the phone rings. A pleading voice begs for advice. The years pass, and instead of motherhood ending, it begins a new role with another title: Grandmother. Same loving, same nurturing, same prodding in the right direction — only with a bit more spoiling.

At some point it may appear you've changed roles completely, as your now grown child mothers you. Not so. Because inside, where it really counts, a mom never changes: she's always guiding, always giving, always loving ...

Just like our heavenly Father.

DAY-BREAK

Think about when your role switched from "Mom" to "Grandmom." How did you first find out? How did you feel? Overwhelmed? Overjoyed? Worried? Fearful?

DAY-BRIEF

God — and his love for us — never changes.

DAY-VOTEDLY YOURS

Father, thank you for your faithfulness daily. Help me in this new role as a grandmother to mirror your love to my children and grandchildren. I need your wisdom as I begin yet another great adventure in my life.

day 2
what's in a name?

And I will do whatever you ask in my name,
so that the Father may be glorified in the Son. You may ask me
for anything in my name, and I will do it.
John 14:13 – 14

When my husband and I learned we would soon be grandparents, we casually discussed with our children what the grandkids might call us. I ruled out some common names like "Grandma," "Grandmama," "Granny," and "Grandmommy," since they reminded me of my own or my husband's grandparents and great-grandparents.

My girls agreed. So I suggested "Mimi," and my husband selected "Papa." They just sounded good together.

Somewhere in the discussion my husband announced some no-no names: forget about "Pe-po," "Po-Po," or "Paw-Paw." Or "Me-ma," I added for myself. By this time, we were on a roll. Then Larry remembered one more name from an old Jimmy Stewart rerun where Jimmy's grandkids called him "Boom-paw."

"Whatever you do, don't call me Boom-paw."

Big mistake. As the birth date grew closer, one of our sons-in-laws decided to have some fun. Every email and card began with "Dear Boom-paw." Mercifully, however, the name began to fade, and my son-in-law used it only occasionally. The four grandkids have stuck to "Mimi." But Papa didn't win out completely. Our "boom-paw" son-in-law's second child, Lauren, pronounced her own version of Papa's name. He promptly became "Pop-pops" to her.

I've talked to other grandmoms about the origin of their names. Many, like me, chose them. Some children stated their preference without giving the grandparents a choice. But a large number of women live with the nicknames their grandchildren called them early on. I imagine that's where all those, um, "unique" names originated. Eager to pronounce the name for the one they loved, little tongues started calling them an affectionate title long before they understood the meaning. Their motive was, no doubt, love. And in reality, we as grandmoms don't mind at all.

I thought about that recently. What's in a name? Why had I chosen "Mimi"? Larry really couldn't have cared less what the kids called him, even if it was "Boom-paw." But I wondered about my real motive in choosing my name. "Mimi" sounded younger, more modern, and somehow not as "old" sounding as some old-fashioned names. Perhaps it was my way of rebelling at the realization I was growing older.

But whatever the initial motive, that name has become strangely personal. When my grandchildren approach me, they are still young enough to run to me in childlike innocence and adoration: "Miiiiiimiiiiiii!" as they throw eager arms around my neck. At the pronouncement of my special name, my heart melts. There are other women named "Mimi." But my grandchildren's name for me is different, because they *know* me personally. At that moment, I think I would do anything for my grandchildren.

> *Knowing about Jesus and really knowing him personally are two different things.*

What's in a name, really? Apparently a lot, according to God's Word. Throughout Scripture, God's name was to be spoken reverently, with a holy hush. When God sent his Son, Jesus, that name would open up the way to a personal relationship with God. We could then "approach God's throne of grace with confidence" (Hebrews 4:16).

Knowing about Jesus and really knowing him personally are two different things. When Jesus said, "Ask in my name," he didn't mean you could wrap your finger around God's heart hoping to receive any *selfish* desire. He was referring to the power of that *personal* name.

When we run to Jesus with open arms of adoration and faith, when we cry out his name because we know him personally, God will do anything on our behalf that will ultimately bring glory to him. The name of Jesus literally moves heaven to earth.

It's all in the Name.

DAY-BREAK

How do you approach God? Do you know Jesus personally? Write down what his name really means to you.

DAY-BRIEF

At the name of Jesus, all of heaven stops to listen.

DAY-VOTEDLY YOURS

Jesus, your name means so much to me. How many times have I cried to you, and you have answered me? May I never take your name for granted, Lord Jesus. I really want to know you even more.

back to the present

They seldom reflect on the days of their lives,
because God keeps them occupied with gladness of heart.
Ecclesiastes 5:20

"Grandmom, what's the matter with your face?" A small child, see-ing her grandmother deep in thought, began to run her fingers over the lines in her grandmother's face, then traced the frown on her lips. The woman looked annoyed and just shook her head at her little granddaughter.

We all experience times when our minds seem to drift to another time and place. Reflection, in the sense of self-examination, is good, unless it turns to self-absorption. How easy it is to get stuck in the past, remembering only the painful moments of our lives. When that happens, what others may see — including our grandchildren — are hard hearts and sour faces. Smiles turn to permanent frowns, and repetitive beauty treatments can't begin to erase the wrinkles of worried, worn hearts. That kind of reflection helps no one.

But when God consumes our hearts, the reflections step up to a higher plane. How does that happen?

It happened to me one morning when I woke up grumpy and depressed. I reviewed my journal only to uncover a negative pattern emerging. Whines and whimpers lined the pages of my recent entries. *Show me the happy moments of my past, Lord,* I prayed. *Refresh my memory of the faithful journey we've taken together. Please, restore my joy!*

The next morning I grabbed my pen and exchanged an older journal for my long neglected "Blessing Catcher" and started writing. Faithfully, God began to answer my cry. Childhood snapshots, sweet pictures of a young mom, and joyful scenes from the past I'd long since forgotten flooded my memory. Laughter bubbled up from somewhere deep inside, as if loosed from its pent-up prison.

I began to record all the ways God had blessed me in recent days and months. God gently reminded me of the hope and future he had planned for me. Through his eyes, I saw the expectant faces of my grandchildren — and how they might see me in those negative times.

God loves our honesty. He cares about how we feel. But he wants to give us joy.

That experience grew into a frequent practice. From that point on, my reflections of the past included generous reminders of God's grace and blessing. Oh, sure, I still complain some in my journals. Body aches, temporary distractions, too little sleep, and difficult circumstances can easily affect even our spiritual equilibrium as grandmothers. But just as David did so regularly in the Psalms, by the end of my journal entry, I can enter the awesome presence of the Lord again. God loves our honesty. He cares about how we feel. But he wants to give us joy.

Once God has freed us from any negative patterns and shown us his lessons from the painful part of our past (and that's an important part of the process), we won't have time — nor do we want to *take* time — to reflect on mistakes or injustices except to momentarily thank God for teaching us a better way and moving us on! God will keep us too busy counting — and recounting — our joyful blessings now for us to waste time wallowing in unhealthy self-absorption about the past.

Even our grandchildren will notice the difference.

DAY-BREAK

Are painful memories hindering your present joys? Take time to tell God about them. If it helps, write it down. Then make a list of all the things you can celebrate now.

DAY-BRIEF

Even in unchangeable circumstances, God can change our in-look — and our outlook.

DAY-VOTEDLY YOURS

Lord, life is too brief to grump my way through. You are so patient and loving. Thank you for all the times you've helped me in the past. From now on, fill my heart with miles of smiles!

day 4
bridging the grandmother gap

She speaks with wisdom, and faithful instruction is on her tongue.
Proverbs 31:26

As grandmothers, it's easy to get caught up in "the way we raised *our* kids," or "When I was a girl, I used to walk five miles in the snow to get to school" mindset. Even if you're raising your own grandkids — and many of you are — your repetitive (and boring) comments may only bring a roll of their eyes and a chuckle behind your back. What do they care? Wait a minute. Shouldn't they care?

Yes and no. That really isn't the issue. It's all about relating and communicating to your grandkids and the generation in which they live. Examine your motive. Are you trying to point out your grandkids' ingratitude? To pat yourself on the back? To teach a lesson? There are better ways.

My friend Judy Senter invited her grandkids every summer to a week of "Camp JuJu." In that fun atmosphere, she blended a healthy dose of wisdom from the past and familiar activities for the present. The result? The kids couldn't wait for Camp JuJu! In those magical moments of summer, they transformed their grandmother JuJu into a hero who knew how to relate — and demonstrate — love to her grandkids. Judy didn't even live in the country, though she often took the kids special places. She respected the kids' unique abilities and parental training, but she didn't hesitate to share her own experiences through creative hands-on activities.

When visiting my young grandson one year, I decided to try my own version of blending the past and present and invited him to go on a backyard "treasure" walk. I wanted my grandkids to enjoy outdoor nature as I often had as a child. I wasn't prepared for the toddler's comments: "Yuck! These leaves aren't treasures. They're dead." Hmmm.

Recently we were again visiting with my grandson, now almost kindergarten age. This time all four of the grandkids — all under age five — were present. It was my wise husband — and my own children — who taught me something about bridging this grandmom gap. Early one morning after breakfast, my husband opened the front door of my daughter's house and said with great animation, "Come here, kids, I want to show you something."

The three oldest charged outside, running in all directions. "What? Where?" they cried, almost in unison. "I don't see anything."

"Shh! Come back on the porch and listen. Shh! Do you hear that?" Silence. Somehow when Papa speaks, the kids listen. And in a beautiful symphony that only God could create in the city, we heard a chorus of birds, singing their greeting to welcome the early morning.

*Our grandkids will never outgrow
the size of our hearts.*

I moved into the middle, determined to keep the magical spell alive that Papa had cast. We both pointed out the different kinds of birds and how their songs were as unique as their names. "God made those birds!" we added. "Don't you love their music?"

The moment lasted, well, only a moment. But thirty minutes later I chuckled when all of us donned our tennis shoes and headed out on a "treasure walk," led by Papa. Papa was smart. He didn't call it that. He simply asked, "Who wants to go for a walk?" But he made sure that our grandson took his nifty bug catcher, a gift from Mom and Dad (also smart). Even the granddaughters enjoyed scooping up those bugs and momentarily suspending their tiny, fragile bodies on a magnifying glass — before mercifully letting them go.

Judy's grandkids have outgrown Camp JuJu, and ours will soon abandon treasure walks. But they will never outgrow the size of our hearts. They're big enough to make way for a future generation.

DAY-BREAK

How do you communicate your past experiences with your grandkids? What bridges can you build to narrow the grandmother gap?

DAY-BRIEF

Yesterday is not a measure of success, but a bridge to God's new adventures.

DAY-VOTEDLY YOURS

Father, teach me your ways, and purify my motives. When wisdom is lacking, show me creative ways to connect with my grandchildren. Let them see Jesus in me.

the tie that bonds

There is a time for everything . . .
a time to weep and a time to laugh.
Ecclesiastes 3:1, 4

I had never heard of Beanie Babies, but the year Mother came to visit my sister and me in Texas, I learned they had both been following this new craze with rabid interest. They were in it for the investment, they said.

Out of curiosity during that visit, I decided to go on a "hunt" with them both. I'd go and help *them* find some Beanies. What would that hurt? It would just increase the bond with my mom and sister — and maybe even my grandchildren who would soon be born. After all, I could buy a few to keep as gifts for them.

A friend had alerted me that a shipment of furry creatures was due the very next morning. So the three of us staked out the local Hallmark, then drew up a plan. The next morning, we rose with the sun. With our Beanie game faces on we prepared for the "hunt." What luck! We arrived early, with adrenalin pumping, and netted a prime place before the store opened — near the head of the line. In time, the other eager shoppers snaked all the way up the sidewalk.

The Beanie Babies had names, and I had studied up some the

night before to see what was hot and what was not. So when the doors opened, like bulls out of a chute, we rushed in, each grabbing a basket. What happened next completely washed away any quiet, dignified image of grandmothers (of which we all qualified in age). Seeing all those adorable, tagged creatures took its toll on me. I snapped. The hunt was on, and in a matter of seconds, I was hooked. We all started stuffing our baskets with furry critters.

Suddenly I saw a red creature, a furry bull — one of those "hot" Beanies for which we were searching. "I found a SNORT!" I squealed.

"I'll take a SNORT!" yelled my sister. And then my eighty-something mother chimed in, "I'll take TWO SNORTS"!

> ### *Sharing light moments with those we love increases the joy of relationship.*

As every head turned toward us, I gave thanks silently that none of my church members were present on this hunt to witness our outbursts. Because by this time, we were "snorting" and hooting like crazy, bent over, with tears running down our faces.

Years have passed since then, and so has the Beanie craze, but the bond God created that day between the three of us grew to a new level.

My mother died last year. So we began the necessary, painful process of sorting through her things. But as we uncovered her collections of unsold Beanies, we shared fresh tears and laughter at the memories of those crazy Beanie hunts.

Some people think grandmothers only wear frowns and

wrinkles. God says there's a time for everything. Sharing light moments with those we love increases the joy of relationship. Mom taught us that there's no age limit to having fun!

DAY-BREAK

How do you "lighten" up your days? What can you do to keep a joyful spirit? Do your grandchildren see you having fun?

DAY-BRIEF

Burdens grow lighter when relationships grow sweeter.

DAY-VOTEDLY YOURS

Lord, put a smile on my heart. Sweeten my relationships with joyful moments, and keep me ever close to you.

day 6
the grandmother prayer

Father ... I pray for them ... I have made you known to them,
and will continue to make you known in order that the love you have
for me may be in them and that I myself may be in them.
John 17:1, 9, 26

Just before his death and resurrection, Jesus prayed a long, intense prayer for his present — and all future — disciples. Taking Jesus' prayer as our inspiration, my husband and I prayed for our children and grandchildren — our "little disciples" — long before their birth. At one of my daughter's baby showers, I shared in a special prayer time for her and her first baby as we gathered around her.

The tears flowed as friends and family members laid gentle hands on Jen and prayed for God's blessings for every phase of the birth. Sweet prayers mingled like fresh perfume, and I imagined them ascending, special delivery, to heaven on the wings of snow-white doves.

But I wanted to do more. Years of fervent praying and fasting for our own children's needs had ignited an urgency to continue the pattern for my own grandchildren. Before the birth of each one, I decided to document those prayers and send them to each grandchild. I have tried to personalize each grandchild's prayer and avoid a one-size-fits-all for each one, though some thoughts apply to them all. When they grow old enough, whether I am still living or not, they will know the heart behind their grandmother's prayers.

Here's a sneak peak at just a few words from those lengthy prayers:

"You don't know me yet, but you will one day. I know you, though. I know you through your mother's eyes and heart. I've prayed for you for so long! I prayed that you would be the apple of God's eye and that you would be a woman after God's own heart. Ephesians 3:17 – 19 became a frequent request for you.

"I am praying that your hands will always be reaching upward in praise and thanksgiving to your heavenly Father, and outward to those around you as you bless them with his love. I am praying that your feet will always run swiftly to his arms and that you will follow in his steps. I'm praying that when you fall, you will get up again with eyes on the Father who keeps loving you in the right direction.

"I am praying that the eyes of your heart will always be open to Jesus and to the needs of others, just like your mom and dad's are. I am praying that your lips will always speak truth, and that your faith will grow as big as an oak with roots drawing nourishment daily from the Father's own water source. I am praying you will always be hungry for him, hungry to know him, and that you will fall in love with Jesus over and over and over again. And yes, I am praying for you to grow up and be just like him.

*A grandmother's prayers are priceless gifts
you can give away at any age or stage.*

"I pray that your thirst for knowledge and goodness and beauty will thrive and that you will always use your many gifts to bless the Father who loves you so much. I pray you will come to know deeply, fully, completely how unique you are and how awesome God is — and that you indeed are his visible image on earth."

Only God knows the powerful force of prayer. Scores of people trace their success back to the fervent pleas of a grandmother on her knees. And grandchildren never outgrow their need for your prayers.

I've heard it said that grandkids are God's second chance to us for raising children. Whether you're working on getting it right the second time or just extending a practice that began with your own kids, a grandmother's prayers are priceless gifts you can give away at any age or stage.

The best thing about a grandmother's prayers is that they bring heaven — and your grandchildren — a little closer to your heart.

DAY-BREAK

How do you pray for your grandchildren? What would you like to visualize for them? Write a note this week to each grandchild telling them you are praying for them, and for what specific things you are asking God to do in their lives.

DAY-BRIEF

A grandmother's prayers — and tears — will always outlive her years.

DAY-VOTEDLY YOURS

Jesus, keep my grandchildren near to your heart. Make them disciples growing up into godly men and women someday. Prompt me daily to pray for their needs and concerns, and never let me forget how special they are to me and to you.

re-tearment

But with God all things are possible.
Matthew 19:26

*The years have come and gone, and now we're settling in
    again;*
*It's time to build some dreams, and stop looking where we've
    been.*
But just about the time we start to get a second wind,
We find our grown-up children are moving home again.

Sound familiar? It does to Barinda. This senior adult had just completed the papers that would activate her Social Security payments. And her long-time teaching career had ended with the beginning of her retirement benefits. Barinda had dreamed of retirement for years, haunting the travel agencies for possible trips and tours. White-sand beaches, turquoise waters, ancient wonders, and snow-covered peaks — she wanted to experience them all.

But two weeks after Barinda's official retirement began, her life took a drastic turn. Barinda's daughter Maylan, a single parent who had never married, was arrested on a drug bust. A robbery went awry; a policeman was killed, and Maylan faced a felony charge — with possible life imprisonment.

The news itself shocked Barinda, but more details followed.

The courts determined Grandmother Barinda was the only living relative in good health that could properly care for — and raise — Maylan's six-year-old son. Five years earlier, the death of Barinda's husband to cancer had left her a widow.

Once again, life handed Barinda a huge question mark. What's a grandmother to do?

What she has to, of course. Barinda's task seemed insurmountable at times, but she accepted her grandson with all the love that a grandmother's heart could give. She surrendered her dreams and asked God to give her new ones.

Unfortunately, we don't get to write the script for our lives. If we could, we would no doubt eliminate the unpleasant circumstances. I'm sure Barinda's retirement to-do list never included, "Fix lunch for my grandson. Go to the PTA meeting at 5:00. Help grandson with science project. Plan birthday party. Teach him how to have a quiet time and how to be a godly young man. Attend basketball games. Talk to him about dating etiquette. Help him fill out scholarship applications." But God is more interested in changing us than in changing our circumstances, though sometimes he does both.

God is more interested in changing us than in changing our circumstances, though sometimes he does both.

Another woman, much older than Barinda, never experienced retirement either. At the time most women enjoyed rocking their great-grandchildren, Sarah bore a baby boy, God's promised child to Sarah and Abraham. Can you imagine the taunts and stares she would face if nurses wheeled her through the hospital exit today with a newborn on her lap? "Hey, Grandma, did someone switch moms at birth? Don't break any bones changing diapers!" (Genesis 21:1 – 6).

Sarah's to-do-list may have worn her out (although servants helped). She never lived long enough to see or know her grandchildren (Genesis 23:19; 24:1 – 4). One thing is for sure. God walks beside us every step of the way, just as he did with Sarah and Abraham.

Your life as a grandmother may require a 180-degree turn, superhuman strength, and a heart of unconditional forgiveness. God may revise your grandmother title to Mother again if your grown children — or your growing grandchildren — move back in with you. A grandmother's dreams for retirement don't usually include raising a child in the senior years of life. And "This too shall pass" offers little comfort when you realize you may "pass on" by the time the situation "passes."

But age is not a factor with God. Many still believe that dreams belong to the young at heart. "They are the hope of the future, the visions of success," they cry. No matter how old or young, dreams are born — and reborn — in the lives of those who refuse to surrender to mediocrity, in the hearts of those who accept life as an exciting challenge, and in the minds of those who dare to press on regardless of the circumstances.

To those willing to receive, God offers a fresh, daily supply of supernatural power, strength, and grace. With him, all things really are possible.

Just ask Sarah.

DAY-BREAK

What dreams do (did) you have for retirement? Has God altered those in any way? In what areas has "grandmother" included some unexpected turns?

DAY-BRIEF

God makes all things possible, plausible, and passable.

DAY-VOTEDLY YOURS

God, no matter what the future brings, I want to thank you ahead of time. Help me not to cling to my dreams, so that if you decide to change them, I can surrender them quickly.

long-distance discipleship

Therefore go and make disciples.
Matthew 28:19

I wanted to influence my grandchildren in a positive way and to add to the biblical foundation my children were already building in their kids' lives. Letters and prayers and occasional emails helped express my love across the miles, but what more could I do? Our ministry life didn't include the blessing of living near our grown children and their families. Long-distance discipleship presented a challenge.

One day I hit on an idea that would accomplish two purposes. Unfortunately, I had been sucked into the Beanie Baby-collecting craze years ago at the peak of its frenzy. (Remember how I told you my mom and sister introduced me to them?) The trendy "investment" opportunity, however, left me holding the bag — lots of bags — of Beanies. I planted furry critters in hospital gift bags, decorated my office with them, sent many packing to Mexico missions, and sold a few. Still, I had so many.

That's when I decided to use them to sort of "build character" in my grandchildren. *That certainly involves discipleship*, I reasoned. I'm sure their parents loved the idea too, especially when hot pink or chartreuse green critters ended up on a red or navy bedroom ensemble.

I studied my grandchildren on our few visits and listened to their parents' stories of how they had grown through the months. I tried to pick out Beanie Babies that would somehow "match" a character quality in my grandkids. Of course, for preschoolers, that took a little visual imagination.

I called it the "Beanie Baby Character Club." Teddy bears symbolized love and a caring nature; puppy dogs represented loyalty and faithfulness. A kangaroo with her baby stood for a nurturing spirit, and chicks exhibited eagerness. Because the company gave its Beanie Babies name tags and "birth dates," I tied in the special name with my choice of character quality and often used the accompanying birth date, if appropriate, especially if that happened to be the birthday of my grandchild or the year of their birth.

I told my grandchildren initially that these animals could also be called "Pass-it-on" Beanie Babies. Why? Because they needed to pass the furry pets on to someone else when their bedroom "zoo" overflowed with too many creatures — and when they tired of playing with them. In this way, I hoped to encourage generosity.

We as grandmothers are like cheerleaders, affirming our grandchildren's strengths, acknowledging their efforts, and applauding their successes.

I typed the character quality and included my assessment of how my grandchildren were growing and learning that month's character quality. I encouraged them to keep that characteristic alive as they grew in Jesus, and I gave them an appropriate Scripture verse to remember — one using that particular character quality. I printed these on a sheet of parchment, cut to a smaller paper size, and then laminated them at the local printer. Then each month I sent my grandchildren a "character" Beanie Baby with their own special note. At least that was the plan.

Life filled and months passed, and I neglected to send them their monthly character Beanies after a few times. But I kept a big bag full of Beanie Babies in my home office. I discovered in the process that my grandkids preferred picking out their own critters, so whenever they came to visit, I let them stuff as many into their suitcases as their parents would allow.

At least one part of the plan worked — but not because of my creativity. My grandchildren have grown in character because God — and their parents — are doing a great job of intentional parenting and discipleship.

Unfortunately, my stash of "character" Beanie Babies kept growing. The supply seemed endless. But I needn't worry. God himself has an effective and endless supply of discipleship help available. He is in the business of building character. His Word is like a lamp and a path that leads to godly truth and actions. And we as grandmothers are like cheerleaders, affirming our grandchildren's strengths, acknowledging their efforts, and applauding their successes.

Whether your grandchildren live in the next state or next door, God has a plan for all of his kids to make their "characters" more like him. And when God is in charge, it's in the "bag."

P.S. If you need help building character in your grandchildren, I still have plenty of "characters" available for purchase.

DAY-BREAK

How are you involved in helping to "disciple" your grandchildren? Is your current role a cheerleader, trainer, or coach? What can you do to support your children in their parenting efforts to build character in your grandchildren?

DAY-BRIEF

Only God builds character. We just supply the raw ingredients.

DAY-VOTEDLY YOURS

God, thank you for the way you build character in each of us, firmly disciplining, gently prodding, and actively discipling. Grant me wisdom to know how I can support my own children in the important task of discipleship.

day 9

it all comes back to him

Do not fear, for I am with you; do not anxiously look about you,
for I am your God. I will strengthen you, surely I will help you.
Isaiah 41:10 (NASB)

You would think by the time we're grandmothers, we'd have this fear thing under control. How many times did we cry "Help!" to God when we were moms, shaking in our shoes? You name it, we feared it — for ourselves and for our kids during the child-rearing days. *Will I make it through childbirth? Will we both survive the teen years? Lord, don't let them get hurt! Will they pull through this illness?*

I remember one fear that gripped me so tightly I struggled with it for months. As a young mom, I dreaded when my husband, Larry, would leave for overnight conventions or weeklong mission trips. What if he didn't return? How would I make it through the years with small kids? What if something happened to him?

And then one night when Larry was away, I dreamed someone was lifting me out of bed, carrying me far away from my children and my home. I woke up crying, "Jesus! Jesus! Where are you?" Immediately, I felt his warm presence surrounding me and strong arms sustaining my trembling body. That night I gave my husband to God, realizing I had no control and no power of my own to prevent anything from happening to him. He belonged to God, not me.

Like all moms, I've experienced many other fears since that time, but never again did I wrestle with that particular phobia. And one by one, God has eliminated numerous fears as my children grew into adulthood.

So I wasn't expecting the emotions that welled up in me one day when I was visiting my pregnant daughter, who lived several hundred miles away. In a few months I would change my status from "Mom" to "Mimi," as a brand-new grandmother. I was ready, wasn't I?

We had been shopping for new baby things together at a Wal-Mart only hours before I heard the news. I had helped Jen unload the basket, then pushed the cart down to its designated "parking" place. She waddled around to the front seat; we buckled up and left for home.

On the six o'clock news I heard the breaking story: A young mother of two small children — a preschooler and an infant — had just unloaded her shopping cart. She was buckling the oldest child in the car and had her back turned to the infant, who was resting inside his car seat in the cart. Before the mother could spring into action, a woman had stopped her car, jumped out, and grabbed the baby and the car seat, and sped off. The young mom ran after her, grabbing on to the woman's car door, until the car jerked away, leaving the mom screaming for her baby.

A bystander later reported that they had seen the car circling for several minutes earlier as if watching for a possible target.

God is big enough to wrap his protective arms around your loved ones.

That was the same store and the same parking lot where my daughter and I had been only hours earlier — the same one where she would be shopping with her infant in only a few months. Without warning, fear rose up in my pre-grandmother heart, and I realized that not even grandmoms are exempt from anxiety.

We heard later that police had found the woman and the baby, and they had returned the infant, unharmed, to the desperate mom. But the good news didn't relieve my fears.

After we returned home the next day, I realized there was nothing I could do to protect my future grandchildren from harm other than to pray constantly. But that experience drew me back into the arms of my heavenly Father, where I had found comfort for so many years as a woman and a mom.

Whether you are raising your own grandchildren or live miles away from them, you can never escape the temptation to anxiously look about you, fearing for your children and grandchildren's safety. The world we live in will fuel that tendency daily. But God has not taken a vacation. He's still there with you. And he's big enough to wrap his protective arms around your loved ones as well.

His strength will sustain you. And in time, those fears will fade as you rest in a God whose track record of faithfulness is indisputable.

DAY-BREAK

What new fears have crept into your life since becoming a grandmother? How has God helped you through those times? What will you do the next time you are tempted to "look about anxiously"?

DAY-BRIEF

Fear is when we look around instead of up.

DAY-VOTEDLY YOURS

Heavenly Father, you've seen me through years of fears — and you've dried all my tears. What makes me think you'd stop now? I reaffirm my trust in you, my faithful God.

the love factor

But the greatest of these is love.
1 Corinthians 13:13

I anticipated their questions long before my first grandbaby arrived. Both of my daughters started asking a few during their pregnancies. But what could I tell them? Both would shop for baby clothes in their thirties. I gave birth to both of them in my early twenties.

I'm not sure they were really impressed with my tales of a forty-two-hour labor when they both sailed through a maximum of two whole hours of intense labor pain (or less). Or that I somehow managed to survive through seven weeks of severe postpartum depression with my first child, with less than three hours of sleep a night, nursing, and on prescribed sleeping pills (what were we all thinking?).

What advice could I really offer? I called the doctor if my baby's temperature jumped past 99 degrees. Wouldn't my remedies be outdated? As a mom, I was young, inexperienced, and seemed to learn everything the hard way — through trial and terror. Was I really cut out for this grandmother role now? Would I remember how to take care of grandkids when my girls asked me to keep them at times? After all, God didn't bless us by living close to each other. I wouldn't be able to call them across town for a quick rescue when I babysat. They could be on a getaway trip miles — or oceans — away.

Nevertheless, when the grandbabies were born, my daughters continued their questions. I answered the best I could. But sometimes I literally couldn't remember what I'd done in certain situations. Many times I'd revert to this: "Your mother's instinct will kick in and you'll usually know what's best for your child, even if you can't figure out the exact problem at the moment. What babies really need is to be loved, to be fed, to stay dry, and to get lots of sleep."

I introduced solid food to my babies early on. My daughters didn't spoon-feed theirs until much later. As babies, they slept on their stomachs. Through the years doctors changed their minds about that, so my grandbabies slept on their backs. I'm sure my girls didn't need all my creative suggestions on how to entertain small kids on long road trips. Their kids watch *Cinderella*, *Dora*, and *Cars* on portable DVD players.

In spite of my doubts and inadequacies, I soon learned that some things never change. The first time I held the first grandbaby in my arms, sweet memories of motherhood surged through my mind and heart. And each time I held a newborn grandchild, as I felt their fine, fuzzy hair and soft, velvety skin against my cheek, and as they wrapped their tiny fingers around my own, it all came back to me. No, not answers to my daughters' questions. What worked in my generation might be considered taboo today.

God equips every grandmother with the same natural instincts she's always had.

What God reminded me of were those basic needs: to be loved, to be fed, to stay dry, and to get lots of sleep. As a new "Mimi," I contributed what I could to those basic things when I could spend a little time with them — but I concentrated mostly on the "love" need.

Whether it seems like just a few years or a lifetime since you first left the hospital as a new mom, and whether you're up on the latest mothering techniques or not, there's one thing you can be sure of: God equips every grandmother with the same natural instincts she's always had.

A little love goes a long way.

DAY-BREAK

If you had daughters, what kinds of questions did they ask you about raising kids? Describe your emotions the first time you held your new grandchild. Write your daughter or son today and tell them how proud you are of them and what a great parent they are.

DAY-BRIEF

Some questions can only be answered with a hug.

DAY-VOTEDLY YOURS

Lord, I may not know much, but I know I love you, my kids, and now my own grandchildren. Help me to love them as you have loved me.

day 11
the certainty of uncertainty

The LORD gave and the LORD has taken away;
may the name of the LORD be praised.
Job 1:21

My husband woke up one morning and announced to me: "I've made a decision today. I'm going to retire at fifty-five, grab the money, and run!"

Only one small problem. It was his birthday (he had just turned fifty-five), and there was no money to grab — and no place to run to, even if he were serious.

Over 78 million Baby Boomers will soon be eligible for retirement. I wonder how many of them plan to declare the same thing, only with a different age goal: "I'm going to retire at sixty-six, grab the money, and run!" But with recent financial disasters, many no longer know *what* date to project for retirement, if any. Some are thinking, "Will I ever save enough for that elusive dream?"

As a grandmother — young or old — you may be one of those asking similar questions. How do I plan? Will I still have a job? How long should I work? What will I do? Where on earth will I get the money? What if something happens to my husband? If you're a single grandmother or have serious health issues, your fears may double in proportion as you realize no one is contributing to your savings or retirement account but you.

Even if you are currently drawing Social Security and consider yourself already retired, your question may be, "Should I look for a job? And who's hiring white-haired grandmas, anyway?"

Common concerns — and certainly serious ones. Some of you may have lost 20 to 30 percent of your retirement savings in past stock market plunges or bank failures. But more troubling to you than anything is the fact that not even the best financial experts can predict the future. And no, not even the government can rescue you with a "grandmother bailout plan." In reality, hasn't it always been that way (in terms of knowing the future)?

If we want not only to survive, but also to thrive as women and grandmothers, we need to think big — bigger than what we see, feel, or hear from Washington, the media, or financial gurus. Certainly, you and your spouse need to plan responsibly and listen to solid, grounded advice. My friend Ellie Kay offers some great financial counsel and biblical principles in her books, including *Living Rich for Less*, as do other experts like Ron Blue and Dave Ramsey. Don't expect God to act on your behalf if you haven't done your part in handling your finances with godly principles.

But what happens when the best plans go awry, no matter how wise you've been? Wealth can vanish in a moment. Events like September 11, 2001, remind us that life is fragile and uncertain. There are no certainties.

Except one. A man name Job discovered that in the midst of loss. In one day, he lost more than most anyone could endure, even in the worst depression: most of his wealth and all of his children, crushing the hopes of any grandchildren for him and Mama Job. As if that weren't enough, his health evaporated. In spite of all his careful planning and faithfulness to God, life turned on him like a bloodthirsty terrorist. Yet he clung to a certainty that helped sustain him: "I know that my redeemer lives, and that in the end he will stand on the earth" (Job 19:25).

Friends tried to influence Job's thinking, accusing him of ignorance, pride, and even presumption (Job 8:8–9; 15:5–6; 22:23). They ignored the truth found in Job 1:22: "In all this, Job did not sin by charging God with wrongdoing." Job wasn't perfect or sinless; he just didn't blame God for his losses, and he was a man who trusted God. But in reality, he had no explanation — and no real solutions.

As it turned out, that wasn't necessary. Even though he said it in the wrong context, one of Job's friends nailed a truth that can help free all of us, no matter what our life status: "How great is God — beyond our understanding!" (Job 36:26).

When God finally spoke to Job, he offered a bigger picture than anyone ever could. Four solid chapters record the proof of God's awesome power, his bigness, and his unsurpassable greatness. Scripture doesn't record whether God ever explained to Job exactly why he allowed Job to lose everything. Whoever wrote the book of Job knew, so we can only guess that Job found out too. But God certainly reminded Job of who was and who always has been in charge — God himself.

We are not, as some suggest, "makers of our own destiny." We are, and always have been, at the ultimate mercy of an all-powerful, omnipotent God. To us women and grandmothers that can sound pretty heavy and unnerving. Will Job's fate be ours too?

> *There is great security in committing our future to him,*
> *no matter which way the Dow goes.*

What was God really trying to say to Job through all of his difficulties? And what can we learn from it, in order to face an uncertain financial future?

Thousands of years later, the apostle James gives us a glimpse at another part of God's character — and maybe what God wanted Job to know about him as well — in James's discussion of the importance of perseverance: "You have heard of Job's perseverance and have seen what the Lord finally brought about. The Lord is full of compassion and mercy" (James 5:11).

In the end, God blessed "the latter part of Job's life more than the former part." Mrs. Job not only had grandchildren; she became a great-great-grandma (Job 42:12, 16).

Does that mean God will do the same for you? Only God knows. Whether he does or not isn't the issue. He *will* meet your needs (Philippians 4:19). In spite of the humbling lessons God taught Job, Job's heart clung to his initial confession throughout his life: My Redeemer lives; God gives, and God takes away. Blessed be the name of the Lord!

God is faithful. God is powerful. God is in charge. God is merciful. There's no uncertainty in those truths. But there is great security in committing our future to him, no matter which way the Dow goes.

That's something you can get up and run with.

DAY-BREAK

What kind of financial plans have you made for the future? How are you dealing with uncertainties that may come? Thank God today that he is in charge. And celebrate his greatness by recommitting your future to him.

DAY-BRIEF

There is nothing bleak about a future committed to God.

DAY-VOTEDLY YOURS

God, I cannot even begin to imagine how great your power is, but I know something of your mercy. In the lean times and the in-between times, you have always provided for me. Thank you for the security of knowing you are in control.

bragging rights

Grandparents are proud of their grandchildren.
Proverbs 17:6 (CEV)

I could spot them a mile away as they approached me with that *look* in their eyes. Before I could escape, they'd whip out those five-by-seven rectangles. I'd simply shake my head and smile.

They'd chase me down at the grocery store, the post office, or the church aisle to make sure I'd seen the newborn grandbaby photos in their brag books. I'd ooh and ah, but I'd keep my thoughts to myself: *They act as if they have the only grandkids in the world.*

Most of them boasted the same: "Isn't he handsome?" "Isn't she beautiful?" It didn't matter if they wanted *me* to say those words first. Grandmothers will usually beat you to the draw if you don't respond at the speed of lightning.

Of course, we moms know that not all newborns are beautiful at birth. Most have red splotches, puffy eyes, wrinkled foreheads — and some, even pointy heads. After all, most of us saw ours right after the doctor slapped their bottoms and introduced them to life (we forget that they were beautiful to us then too). But a few days or weeks make a huge difference in their looks. A few weeks later, the same grandmas are showing us *those* pictures too. *Silly old grandmothers.*

Then I had grandkids. A proud grandmother friend of mine gave me my own five-by-seven rectangle book, and I filled that photo book until it bulged with pictures of my own ... ahem ... newborn grandchildren. And then I deposited that album in my purse or Bible cover so that wherever I went, my brag book traveled with me. "Aren't they beautiful?" I'd announce. Inside I'd think, *If you don't agree with me that they are the most beautiful kids you ever saw, something's wrong with your eyesight!*

I'd chase them down in the grocery store, in the post office, down the church aisle ... you get the picture. I have turned into a silly grandmother. (None of us likes to call ourselves *old* yet, however. That's for everyone else.)

I even wrote a story about our first grandchild, Haley, a Christmas Eve baby. I just know you're all dying to hear it: "And there were in the region of East Texas some future grandparents keeping watch day and night for the arrival of their first grandchild. And the Lord saw it was time, and the phone rang in the middle of the night when the moon was shining brightly. And lo, an angel of a son-in-law announced on the other end of the cell phone: 'I bring you good news of great joy, which will delight us all. For today your long-awaited grandchild is being born at this very moment in a hospital bed in West Texas. And this is what you will find when you travel here tonight: By the time you arrive you will find a babe, your first granddaughter, wrapped in a hospital gown lying in the arms of her mother.'

"And suddenly there came a sound from the grandparents like mighty angel voices, praising God and saying, 'Glory to God in the highest, and on earth, there is peace in our hearts, for God — and we — are pleased.'

"And it came about that when they hung up the phone, the grandparents said to each other and everyone they met, 'We are going to see this miracle that will come to pass, which the Lord has made known to us through our son-in-law.' And they drove with haste to the hospital and found the baby in her mother's arms in the hospital room.

"And when the grandparents saw this, they made known the announcement which had been told them about the child. And they went out everywhere showing their brag book pictures of their newborn granddaughter to everyone who would listen. And all who heard it knew that they, themselves, had the best grand-children that ever lived, but they humored the new grandparents anyway. And the grandparents treasured these memories in their hearts, pondering the awesome faithfulness of a loving God."

God himself has the ultimate bragging rights for the most beautiful child.

We grandmoms can brag all we want, but God himself has the ultimate bragging rights for the most beautiful child. And God does have a "brag book." Those who witnessed the birth of God's own Son wrote about his birth in Luke 2. We call it the Christ-mas story. And no matter how "great" you think your kids or your grandkids are, they'll never compare to the greatest One of all: Jesus. God wants everyone to know about his Son, and he'll pursue man, woman, teen, or child — wherever they are — just so they'll know about the good news of his Son's birth.

And I'm glad to know that God feels the same way as you — or I do — about our grandkids. In fact, he takes pride in and loves all of his kids equally. Technically God has no grandchildren. All those, young and old, who have come to accept his offer of grace and forgiveness through his Son, Jesus, are "born" into his kingdom and given the right to be his children.

Now that's something to brag about.

DAY-BREAK

Tell me about your grandchildren. Oops! I forgot, I can't hear you. What size is your "brag book"? Today, reread the story of Jesus' birth in Luke 2 and celebrate the greatest birth of all.

DAY-BRIEF

Grandchildren and grandmothers go together like jelly and peanut butter.

DAY-VOTEDLY YOURS

Father, thank you for my precious grandchildren. But most of all, thank you for sending your son, Jesus, so that we could all share in your bragging rights as your own kids.

day 13

what's age got to do with it?

Love is as strong as death …
It burns like blazing fire, like a mighty flame.
Song of Songs 8:6

As typical teen sweethearts, one of the things Larry and I anticipated was our sexual relationship after we married. We've always
both enjoyed the physical part of our marriage, but it took years for
us to learn the meaning of true oneness.

We learned that even a strong sexual relationship didn't equal
marriage intimacy. After the first fifteen years of our marriage,
we discovered that we had drifted apart emotionally. We were too
busy to spend much time in heart-to-heart talks or in trying to
bridge the chasm that had begun to form.

God eventually opened our eyes to our lack of true marriage
oneness and deep communication, and we sought Christian counseling. It took hard work as we learned for the first time to express
our true feelings about issues. Anger, hurt, and unfair expectations often erupted, but we kept working on our relationship.
With God's help, the counselor led us to discover another level of
intimacy we had never known — and it improved our emotional,
spiritual, and yes, even our physical relationship. Not only that, it
fueled a passion for marriage and for helping other couples through
our training as marriage enrichment leaders.

Now, after forty-two years of marriage, the fire is dimming. Not! Who said "seniors" can't have fun? Women of all ages need to keep working on their relationships, no matter how strong they may seem.

How can grandmothers still fan the flames of romance and intimacy in their marriage? How many times you make love is not the issue. I could quote you the statistics for the "norm" in surveys. But who wants to be the norm? That you share life with each other constantly through a spiritual, emotional, and physical oneness, that you are working together mutually to bring each other pleasure, that you care more about meeting your mate's needs than your own — that's what matters.

If you and your husband have never communicated about long-standing hindrances in the past, it's not too late. Past hurts, bitterness, or difficult backgrounds need to be healed for true intimacy to grow. And even current stressful factors like job loss, work pressures, and financial worries can bring isolation or lack of response if you refuse to work through them together. Gray-haired grandparents can still attend marriage conferences.

God wants oneness for your marriage relationship.

Keep your spiritual relationship close too. Dennis Rainey says, "Loneliness and isolation are put to death when a husband and wife pray together regularly. An open, honest relationship with God, in the presence of your mate, is a prerequisite to a mutually satisfying sex life."[1]

You *are* getting older. As a grandmom, you may feel the changes daily, and so does your husband. But it doesn't mean you start buying flannel nightgowns. You may need to adjust your expectations some, but a check-up and frank discussion with your doctor may help alleviate any physical issues you deal with. And, of course, things like serious or chronic illness can affect your relationship. But age alone doesn't mean your sexual desire has to diminish. In fact, it could even soar.

No matter what age you are, keep the romance alive. After our counseling experiences early in our marriage, Larry and I starting operating on principles we heard from friend and evangelist Paul Burleson. We still teach those to others: divert daily (take time to talk and connect every day); withdraw weekly (go on a date every week); and abandon annually (get out of town for special romantic escapes). We love that last one so much that we try to "abandon quarterly" when we can.

Keep doing the things you once did. Revelation 2 has some great truths that can also apply to marriage if you've "lost your first love." Why stop dating, handholding, cuddling, surprising each other, or writing love notes?

One night before Larry got up to preach, I slipped a note into his Bible that said, "You sure are sexy!" He saw it while we were singing a congregational hymn and looked up at me. We got so tickled, I was afraid we'd both have to leave.

We both realize we can never stop working on our relationship if we want it to be what God intended. We want our love for each other to be a gift and example both to our children and to our grandchildren.

God wants oneness for your marriage relationship. It doesn't need to stop growing. Aging doesn't mean the flame is going out. You may just need to put a few more logs on the fire.

DAY-BREAK

How would you describe the "fire" in your marriage relationship? Roaring? Flickering? Reduced to embers? Do something this week to stoke the flames: buy new "nightwear"; plan a surprise; affirm your husband generously and ask him how you can pray for him daily.

DAY-BRIEF

It only takes a spark to rekindle a fire.

DAY-VOTEDLY YOURS

Lord, thank you for giving my mate to me, and for the plan of oneness you created for husband and wife. Teach me how to love daily in little ways as well as big ones.

the new "old"

Even youths grow tired and weary…
*But those who hope in the L*ORD
will renew their strength.
They will soar on wings like eagles;
they will run and not grow weary,
they will walk and not be faint.

Isaiah 40:30 – 31

In my grandmother's Bible, I found an old newspaper clipping, an anonymous reprint several decades old, faded and yellowed with age. Here are some excerpts from that column titled "Youth":

Nobody grows old by merely living a number of years; people grow old by deserting their ideals. Years may wrinkle the skin, but to give up enthusiasm wrinkles the soul. Worry, doubt, self-distrust, fear and despair — those are the long, long years that bow the head and turn the growing spirit back to dust …

You are as young as your faith, as old as your doubt, as young as your self-confidence, as old as your fear; as young as your hope, as old as your despair.

In the central place of your heart there is a wireless

station. So long as it receives messages of beauty, hope, cheer, courage, grandeur and power from the earth, from man and from the Infinite, so long are you young!

When the wires are all down, and all the central place of your heart is covered with the snows of pessimism and the ice of cynicism, then you are grown old indeed, and may God have mercy on your soul.

I've since discovered that Samuel Ulmann, a poet who lived from 1840 to 1924, penned this piece — and that it has inspired all ages, including General Douglas MacArthur, who included it in his seventy-fifth birthday speech. I've read that aged poem often myself.

Turning thirty, forty, or even fifty didn't bother me. Some of your children may have married young. Maybe you took the name "Grandmom" in your forties or even late thirties. But God waited several years to bless my children with their own kids. When I finally became a "grandmother," something clicked inside my brain. *I'm getting old.* I didn't particularly *feel* old, and I didn't really *look* old (then I wondered, what does *old* look like?). The only time I really felt my age was when I crawled out of bed in the morning, eased into bed at night, or when I played too long on the floor with the grandkids — well, okay, maybe a few other times.

But there *are* moments in the day where I feel — young. Perhaps a part of me wants to become a subtle believer in the new age divisions: "50 is the new 30"; "60 is the new 40"; "70 is the new 50"; and "80 is the new 60." Organizations like AARP tried to rush it a little bit. They sent me my card long before I ever turned 50.

In the central part of your heart (the mind)
there must be a core belief: God, the ageless one,
determines how old, old really is.

But I take great delight in hearing what God says about age. It does matter what we *think* about the meaning of old. But that doesn't limit God. Sarah herself, when she overheard a heavenly messenger telling her husband Abe that they would bear a son the following year, laughed and thought, "After I am worn out and my lord is old, will I now have this pleasure?" (Genesis 18:12). Nine months later, Sarah was the poster "child" for advertising that "90 is the new 20," as she gave birth to her son Isaac (Genesis 21:1 – 6). Moses, Joshua, Caleb, and a host of God's leaders spent their greatest years in what we would call "old age."

In the building of Solomon's temple, David had assigned both young and old alike to participate as music leaders and instrumentalists (1 Chronicles 25:8). And the psalmist encouraged the faithful who knew God that they would "still bear fruit in old age" (Psalm 92:14). Throughout the Bible, the young are told to respect their "elders" (1 Peter 5:5). In God's eyes, "old" is a good thing — and has no age minimum or maximum.

Grandmothers are living longer these days, but *how many* years we live isn't as important as *how* we live those years. There is great truth in Ulmann's words, but with an apology to the late poet, I'd like to add an addendum to his familiar poem:

In the central part of your heart (the mind) there must be a core belief: God, the ageless one, determines how old, *old* really is. And what — or who — we believe determines how we will live our lives. There are those who are old who are really young. And there are those who are young who are really old.

If you choose to believe God's promises and not others' standards, if you decide to follow his path and not another's, if you determine to make his name known and not your own, then you will never really grow old.

You will only grow closer, wiser, and more in love — with the One who made you and who renews your strength daily.

DAY-BREAK

How do you define "old"? What makes you feel older than your years (besides chasing grandchildren)? How has God renewed your strength?

DAY-BRIEF

Old is when you stop believing God is ageless.

DAY-VOTEDLY YOURS

God, you are always there to strengthen me when body and mind start to feel "old." Help me to age gracefully — as well as gratefully.

day 15

from the inside out

Be strong and courageous. Do not be afraid; do not be discouraged,
for the LORD your God will be with you wherever you go.
Joshua 1:9

Years ago, I purchased a hammock and hung it between two tall trees in my shady back yard, just to fuel my "romanticism" and to remind me to slow down. There I spent many crisp spring and fall mornings with pen, journal, and Bible in hand. As I watched squirrels scampering through the trees and across the yard, burying their acorns, I also tried to "bury" God's fresh manna in my heart as I read from his Word.

A few years later, we found a place for our old, abandoned porch swing on the back patio. On summer mornings, I nestled there for my daily bread. I need to replace the deteriorating hammock, but I keep it swinging there with its moss-stained threads as a symbol of the simplicity I want to retain in my life.

We live in an area where the ground shifts, even if you do water the foundation of the house regularly. Sometimes when that happens, particularly in seasons of extreme drought, the doors stick and are difficult to open. I had been anticipating the arrival of spring and enjoying the back porch again. But the other day I tried to open the back door, and it stuck so badly that I needed a wrench to turn the top lock. I couldn't do it by myself.

So I've been looking at the outside from the inside, watching the daffodils and irises bloom and longing to bask in the first fruits of spring before the season passes.

At this stage of your life, do you ever feel trapped behind the challenges in your life, whether it's an aging body, shifting finances, increasing work demands, or family losses? It may seem as if God is on the outside and you're looking out from the inside, trying to crack open that door to springtime and a fresh start.

Even in the midst of questionable circumstances, God is with you and will never leave you.

Are you experiencing a drought? Does your time in God's Word seem dull and dry, and do you long for his touch on your life once more? You may even feel as if God has left you hanging, like that empty hammock, because few opportunities come your way anymore to use your God-given gifts. You entertain thoughts like, *Has God abandoned me? Will he use me again? Will he ever open this door so that I can smell, hear, touch, and feel springtime before winter becomes the norm for my life?*

Maybe your grandkids live far away, or they've grown older and don't seem to need you anymore. Neither do your children. Maybe you thought you'd be slowing down by now, but life has only accelerated. Your "symbols" of simplicity, if you had any, are rotting, because you can't get out the "door" to enjoy life more. This wasn't what you had in mind for your "grandmother" years.

But God hasn't forgotten you. Even in the midst of questionable circumstances, he is with you and will never leave you. He is still working out his plan for you.

Joshua faced a huge door — one he could not open by himself. Moses, the leader of God's people, had died, and God gave Joshua the new role to lead the people across the Jordan River into a promised, new beginning. The words he spoke to Joshua apply to grandmothers too.

Don't be discouraged. When it's time, God will open the door. He will be with you. Your job then is simply to walk through that door. Spring will come again, from the inside out.

DAY-BREAK

Do you ever feel as if you are behind a door that is stuck? What are the biggest challenges in your life right now? How are you dealing with them? Memorize Joshua 1:8 today and meditate on its words often. Ask God to help you wait on him.

DAY-BRIEF

When God is with us, fear diminishes, and hope increases.

DAY-VOTEDLY YOURS

God, wherever you are is where I want to be. Thank you for your promise to be with me, wherever I go. Help me to experience springtime in my life again and to trust you for the timing.

a star is born

He determines the number of stars and calls them each by name.
Psalm 147:4

Every grandmother believes her grandkids are true "stars." When Priscilla's daughter, Edie, and son-in-law, John Michael, knew they would have a boy, they began to prepare for their "star" to be born. They bought a Mickey Mouse quilt with stars on it. Using the star theme and Mickey as a theme for their nursery, John Michael used his artistic talent to paint phrases around the room on the wall, like "Hitch your wagon to a Star," "Twinkle, twinkle, Little Star," "When You Wish upon a Star," "The Stars at Night," and "A Star Is Born." They even adorned the ceiling with stick-on stars that glowed in the dark.

Grandmother Priscilla, known as "Modie," said the day finally arrived for her grandson to be born. The other grandparents gathered around the hospital in typical fashion to welcome the anticipated addition to their family. Soon, Elden Kyle was born. One of the proud grandpas circulated some pictures taken immediately after Elden's birth. On the picture he had written his grandson's name and the following words: "A Star Is Born."

Maybe you think that's carrying the pride a little too far — until you look closely and see the reason for those words.

When Priscilla's grandson was born, an unusually shaped birthmark appeared above his nose and between his eyebrows. It was small, about the size of a dime, with five points: the shape of a star.

Elden Kyle has been Priscilla's "star" grandchild in many ways. He is her only grandson, but he is also her only grandchild. With her daughter and son-in-law being educators, Priscilla — a retired teacher herself — took over the daily routines in her grandson's life during the school months from the time he was born. Care began early, usually by 6:30 or so, with breakfast at "Modie's" when Mom or Dad dropped him off — continuing until they picked him up after their school duties ended. Priscilla and Elden Kyle have shared special times together, like trips to the library, walks to the park, and dips in the pool. Priscilla even decorated a room in her home like a pirate's den for Elden Kyle's sleepovers.

> *Every grandmother believes*
> *her grandkids are true "stars."*

When "Pop" (Priscilla's husband, Thurman, and Elden Kyle's grandfather) died suddenly, Elden Kyle was only three years old. But the young boy became a "star" that lit up some of the darkness in Priscilla's life. In many ways her grandson helped ease the transition for her sudden loss, because Elden Kyle filled up her home with comforting love.

Because Priscilla lives around the corner from her daughter, son-in-law, and grandson, she shares in their sweet family times and celebrations. They even include her on family vacations, where she has seen Elden Kyle feed his pirate love firsthand at places like Disney World. (Of course, "Modie" helps pay for the adventures — and loves doing it.)

Now that Elden Kyle attends school, Priscilla adds "homework" to her daily agenda with her grandson. Apparently he is continuing to live up to his "star" image — at least for his loved ones. Recognizing his artistic talent (like his dad), his parents enrolled him in a special art class for kids. Elden Kyle's recent entry, a colorful sunset, in a first grade cultural class on "What Wows You," earned him a trophy — and is one of three entries being considered to win state.

I'm sure every grandmother could share her special stories — and granddads too. God gave Abraham a sneak peek into the future about the far-reaching effects of his covenant promise to Abe, and the number of Abe's "grandchildren," or "offspring." God took him out one clear night and invited him to look at the vast number of stars God had created. "Count the stars," God said, "if indeed you can count them" (Genesis 15:5).

The heavens are like a black "art" canvas, dotted with billions of stars — unknown and unnamed to us. Yet the psalmist declares that God knows exactly how many stars are in the heavens, and he calls each of them by name. It was impossible for Abraham — as it is for us — to number them.

If you asked a grandmother, however, to count the number of stars she sees in her world, she could tell you how many in a heartbeat. She even knows them by name. Just ask her how many grandchildren she has.

DAY-BREAK

How many "stars" can you count in your world? In what ways do you consider your grandchildren as stars? How do you nurture your special relationship with them?

DAY-BRIEF

True stars always reflect the true Light.

DAY-VOTEDLY YOURS

Lord, thank you for the "stars" that shine in my life. Keep growing and nurturing the special relationship I have with my grandkids — and help them always to shine for you.

one big, blended family

From him the whole body, joined and held together
by every supporting ligament, grows and builds itself up in love,
as each part does its work.
Ephesians 4:16

Some tiptoe in. Some run in where even angels dare to tread. A few are clueless as to their role. But none of those grandmothers fit Sharon. Stepping into a blended family can be a challenge. How do you combine those families in a way that brings unity?

Sharon Hogan says even names are a big deal in blended families. When she was trying to decide on her own grandmother name, before the first grandchild was born, she had to consider not just her desires, but the needs and wishes of the rest of the members of their new blended family. Each child had three grandmothers and three grandfathers. Since their names would be reflective of their own personalities and unique attributes, the grandparents all pitched in together to create their individual names.

One was more formal while others were more folksy or quaint. Each name seemed to really fit. One grandmother's name became an oddity as a result of their granddaughters' mispronunciation: "Ganga."

The second grandchild's daddy is notorious for being a

jokester, so there was a twist in Sharon's name as he changed it from "Nana" to "Mana." "I liked it and hoped it meant that I'd be the bread from heaven to my grandchildren!" Sharon said. Later, when her own siblings' children started their families, Sharon's name added still another twist. Her sister-in-law chose "Nana," so Sharon's name became "ShaNana" as a grandaunt.

Sharon says, "Our names as grandparents help tell the story like the body of Christ [his church]. We are all different, but still one because of our unified desires as a family."

In reality, you could say a blended family must work like the body of Christ in many ways. Each one adds their ingredients: unique temperaments, individual gifts, and special perspectives. Like the body of Christ, all grandparents must exercise grace, patience, love, and kindness with each other. Should jealousy, selfishness, or bitterness arise, "family" unity will suffer.

A blended family must work like the body of Christ in many ways.

But working together on names isn't the only way Sharon's family builds unity. They all show up together at birthday parties, holidays, children's sports, dance, or school events. They talk together and pray for each other.

For Sharon, many of the resolutions and workings at blending were "pre-grandmother." Like many blended families, she experienced an adjustment period when she first entered the "stepmother" stage of her life. But that prepared the way for a wonderful transition into grandparenting between all of the members. By that time, they had already established a sense of unity that carried into their abilities to grandparent with oneness of mind. They worked at this because first of all, they love their children, and second, because they love the grandchildren who have entered their lives. Above all, Christ is at the heart of their desires to love all of these gifts from God.

Sharon says an openness and willingness to accept each other can help bring that needed unity to a blended family. "My husband's ex-wife and I hug, talk, and share life in joint events with care and consideration for each other."

How do they accomplish that, you ask? Apart from God's grace, that would be a difficult task. It's a truth all of us in the body of Christ need to remember, whether we have actual "blended" relatives or not.

Sharon offers a key truth that explains how — and why — her family keeps unity: "Because what we share together now is far richer and deeper than what divided hearts in the past."

DAY-BREAK

Whether you are a "step-grandmother" or not, how do you work toward building unity in your family? What can you do this week to help build the body of Christ?

DAY-BRIEF

Unity comes when each views the other person as an equally important member of the body.

DAY-VOTEDLY YOURS

Lord, no matter how many members are in the body, you are the head. Help me to do my part in making the body of Christ — and my family — all you want it to be.

day 18

the diet that works

Taste and see that the LORD is good;
blessed are those who take refuge in him.
Psalm 34:8

Recently in one magazine I counted three different perspectives on "How to Live Longer" — by avoiding certain foods. Yet only last week on the television news, new scientific facts had supposedly proved just the opposite. So what's a healthy diet, anyway?

Life is full of mixed messages when it comes to food. One week, chocolate's deadly. The next week, *dark chocolate* extends your life. Our grandmothers cooked with butter. But doctors said that contributes to heart disease. Now, it's good again, compared to the "plastics" contained in margarine. Food can kill you, or food can help you live. It's all in whom you believe — or trust.

You may adopt the "devil may care" philosophy. You paid your dues and you earned the right to do and eat as you please. After all, we're all going to die eventually. It's a matter of how, and when. And no one really knows that but God, right? So bring on the French fries and shakes!

Some of you may look to Jack Lalanne as your hero. Your goal is to stay fit and healthy until you're at least Jack's age — currently ninety-five — and still going strong. You watch what you eat, and also side with the other "Jack" (Sprat) in the old nursery rhyme — the one who could "eat no fat" (as opposed to his wife, who could eat no lean).

Our doctors ask us probing questions, like: What did your mother and father die of? Are there any serious medical conditions in your family history? So then you wonder, is it "genes" or is it "food" that steals our years? Should I diet — or should I wait — to die?

Regardless of which group you identify with, all of us agree that no one has all the answers. Maybe "moderation in all things" is a fairly safe principle. Experience tells us junk foods aren't the most nutritional. Natural foods and less processing are usually healthier. Most of us at least agree on this: it's true that what we put in our bodies affects us either positively or negatively. Smart deduction, don't you think?

> *God also wants us to taste the "food" he gives us*
> *— a steady diet of rich, spiritual nutrition.*

But there is something that we *can* eat, and no matter how much we indulge, it will only bring positive results. It's not really food for our physical bodies that's of most concern to God. True, our bodies *are* temples of God's Spirit, and we need to treat them accordingly, in honor to him (1 Corinthians 6:19). He expects us to use sound and wise judgment, and he gives us plenty of good choices. But God also wants us to taste the "food" he gives us — a steady diet of rich, spiritual nutrition. "Taste and see," says the

Lord. His food not only tastes good; it's good for us! Sounds like a great, healthy diet!

God's truths — his Word — not only "refresh the soul ... they are sweeter than honey, than honey from the honeycomb" (Psalm 19:7, 10). Time with God and eating the spiritual food only he can give bring the ultimate in satisfaction: "I will be fully satisfied as with the richest of foods; with singing lips my mouth will praise you" (Psalm 63:5).

But the best news is that Jesus is life himself: "I am the bread of life ... the living bread that came down from heaven. Whoever eats of this bread will live forever" (John 6:48, 51).

It's a win-win relationship, and you can trust the One who designed the plan. That kind of diet is never questionable. And it comes with God's own spiritual health guarantee.

DAY-BREAK

What kind of food or health concerns do you have? How do you keep your body fit as the temple of God's Spirit? How is your spiritual health?

DAY-BRIEF

The spiritual food that God gives never grows old or stale.

DAY-VOTEDLY YOURS

Lord, my body and health belong to you. Grant me the wisdom to know what's best for my physical body, but most of all, feed me with your living bread daily. I am so hungry for you!

day 19
beauty secrets

Your beauty ... should be that of your inner self, the unfading beauty of a gentle and quiet spirit.
1 Peter 3:3 – 4

My grandmother used an oatmeal/honey mask to keep her face young and fresh looking. To smooth out wrinkles and keep her hands youthful, she smeared Vaseline on them and slept in gloves. My mother relied on her own beauty secrets, and evidently they worked. When she died at ninety-one, she looked sixty-nine.

Some grandmothers today spend a fortune in cosmetics to look young, or at least younger than their years. For the first twenty-five years of child rearing, we pull our hair out. Then the second half of our lives, we pour "color" back in to hide the few remaining hairs that our kids turned gray. You know I'm only kidding, right? (It wasn't really our kids' fault!)

The first time a wrinkle appears, we grab a new cream or mask in the hopes of plumping up the skin — and sloughing off a few years. And everyone has a new beauty secret to offer. The naturalists say, "Look in your pantry or refrigerator. A little olive oil, honey, fruit, or egg white will bring miraculous results." Beauty experts tout their most expensive and recent wonder product. So you try them all — and usually you'll find something you like. Your beauty treatments may even take years off your looks.

When a new fashion trend emerges, some grandmothers couldn't care less. They'll don their purple hats and red dresses and dance to the tune of "When I Grow Old, I Shall Wear Purple." And others, whether they're "boomer-grams" or "great-grams," are still interested in the latest hairstyles, jewelry, and clothes. The trouble is, birthdays still roll around like clockwork. "Age" keeps accelerating, in one way or another.

The real problem is, you can't do a thing about it. You can't delay the inevitable forever. Beauty eventually fades. Or does it?

God's Word offers another viewpoint — along with some true beauty secrets: "Your beauty should not come from outward adornment, such as elaborate hairstyles and the wearing of gold jewelry and fine clothes" (1 Peter 3:3). Was Peter advocating no makeup, hair-in-a-bun, and sackcloth? No. But those things are unimportant when compared to real beauty. A woman's true beauty comes from within.

A woman's true beauty comes from within.

The beauty that does not fade is a gentle and quiet spirit, and God puts great value on it. Apparently so do husbands, as even unbelievers can be "won over without words" by it (1 Peter 3:1). Even grandmothers need that kind of beauty.

What if you're a widow? True beauty — the kind that God nurtures inside a woman — is not only ageless. It's attractive to all who see her and know her. It's the kind of spirit that refuses to call attention to self. And it describes a woman who is not stingy with her beauty secrets.

God doesn't ask us to abandon outer beauty; rather, he wants us to keep it in the right perspective and to focus more on the inner qualities. Dressing modestly and in good taste is a given. But God doesn't want us to depend on outer appearance for our worth or value or to let those things distract us from our real purpose in life — reflecting the beauty of Christ.

When you're concentrating on God's true beauty, don't be surprised if someone — young or old — observes your unfading beauty and comments on it. They may even tap you on the shoulder and ask: "What's your secret?"

DAY-BREAK

What are your "beauty secrets"? What habits have you formed that help make the outer appearance be a reflection of inner beauty? What disciplines are you exercising to maintain a quiet and gentle spirit?

DAY-BRIEF

Jesus always finds a home where true beauty lives.

DAY-VOTEDLY YOURS

Jesus, create in me a beautiful heart, one that reflects you, through and through. Keep my focus on inner beauty, not on my outward appearance. Help me to develop that quiet and gentle spirit and a beauty that never fades — so others can see you, not me.

day 20

nurturing
what comes naturally

Start children off on the way they should go,
and even when they are old they will not turn from it.
Proverbs 22:6

Some things just come naturally to grandmothers. Most, including Mary Griffin, would agree with the psalmist's words that children truly "are a heritage from the LORD," and "a reward from him" (Psalm 127:3).

Each of Mary's four grandchildren brought an equal "Ooh!" and "Ah!" to her grandmother heart as she held the newborn babes in her arms for the first time. Yet each one turned out remarkably different. As she continues to build friendships with them, those unique differences rise to the top like cream.

Dakota, her seventeen-year-old, is a stand-up comedian. Sometimes Grandma gets to go "roadtrippin'" with him and there is lots of laughter and fun and talk. When Dakota was younger, Grandma and Granddad once took him and his younger brother, Sage, to visit a submarine. Sage managed to lock Dakota in one of the compartments, and Dakota's first words to his brother when he finally escaped were, "If this thing has a plank, then you are walking it!"

Another time on one of their camping sites, Mary had to stop on one of their many walks and let Dakota build a bridge with sticks on the road so the ants could cross.

Mary not only nurtures friendship with her grandkids as they travel; she teaches them about ministry and how to reach out to others. Dakota is the one who visits nursing homes with her and delivers Christmas baskets to other aging grandmothers.

Sage is Grandma's tease — and the adventurous one. He's fourteen and has spent half his life with assorted bandages somewhere on his body. Right now he is in a cast up to his knee from skateboarding. As a small boy, he was the one who brought Grandma bouquets of flowers or weeds. It didn't matter to her which one; he always got Grandma hugs in return. Sage is also their builder. He loves to work with his hands in Granddad's shop building things, but he builds them for Grandma.

> *No matter how different*
> *our grandchildren's personalities, we are blessed*
> *when God gives us as grandmothers the distinct privilege*
> *to invest time in each one.*

Tyler, the six-year-old who belongs to their second son, loves structure. When he was about four, on a visit to Mary's home, she asked him if he wanted an egg sandwich.

His words were, "I'll be right back." Then he ran off to his granddad's office.

In a minute he returned. "Go ahead and fix it, Grandmommy.

Granddad says it won't hurt me." (His parents, Steve and Amy, are very careful about what he eats.)

Tyler's first day of school was perfect. Why? He reported to his parents: "It's cool, Daddy. It is so structured!"

Carson, Mary's eleven-month-old grandson, is Tyler's little brother and their bubbly one. Steve and Amy had so wanted another baby, but it just was not happening. Then Steve ran into a problem with blood flow to his heart and was in and out of the hospital several times. Guess what? Amy came up pregnant shortly after.

People everywhere joined their families in fervent prayers for their son and for Amy's pregnancy. Mary was afraid Carson would be frail with a fretful personality, due to the extreme stress at that time. She had wanted their other three grandchildren to suck their thumbs (a sign of a contented baby to her), but none did. Their grandbaby Carson came out sucking his thumb and turned out a very happy and healthy baby.

In spite of her grandchildren's unique differences, Mary found a way to include them all in a variety of activities. She has built tents inside for the boys on rainy days. Together, they've burnt cookies and laughed about it. She even taught the older ones proper table settings, which at the time they considered pretty cool. Did they take that lesson to heart? No. (Boys will be boys.)

No matter how different our grandchildren's personalities, we are blessed when God gives us as grandmothers the distinct privilege to invest time in each one. Some of us, as moms with our own kids, tried to "start" them off in the "same" direction. True, our responsibility as moms and grandmoms is to lead our kids in the right path toward spiritual maturity and toward a solid relationship with Jesus — with prayers that they will never abandon their faith.

But in terms of the "way they should go," we can also help nurture their natural talents, not forcing them into our parental or grandmother ideals, but guiding their God-given gifts and personalities into creative outlets that individually fit them.

Building friendships together with our grandchildren is a great way to do that.

DAY-BREAK

How are you building friendships with your grandchildren? In what ways do you help nurture their natural gifts and abilities?

DAY-BRIEF

The best way to encourage individuality is to nurture each child equally — but also individually.

DAY-VOTEDLY YOURS

Lord, show me how to invest time wisely into my grandchildren's lives. Help me see their uniqueness so that I can build friendships that will last.

day 21
with a little help from my friends

Go around and ask all your neighbors for empty jars.
Don't ask for just a few.
2 Kings 4:3

What would you do if someone knocked on your door to repossess your home and your possessions? How would you respond?

One woman swallowed her pride and asked for help. One of Elisha's godly prophets died, and his wife ran to tell Elisha that the creditors were coming to take her two sons away and make them slaves. She was desperate.

Elisha asked her a practical question: "How can I help you? Tell me, what do you have in your house?" (2 Kings 4:2).

The woman may have already sold all her possessions to pay down as much of her debt as possible. Perhaps she had few marketable goods left — in fact, only a little olive oil. Elisha's instructions to her may sound a little strange. Why borrow empty jars from her neighbors when all she owned was a small amount of oil herself?

She didn't argue, however, and Elisha insinuated that when she started pouring her oil into all the borrowed jars, something miraculous would happen: the jars would fill up with oil. Her boys scoured the neighborhood, pounding on doors, begging for jars.

When they had gathered up all the containers, the widow closed the door and began pouring, filling up one jar after another. When the oil reached the top of every jar, it stopped flowing.

Once again, the widow ran to the prophet Elisha for further instructions. "Go, sell the oil and pay your debts. You and your sons can live on what is left" (2 Kings 4:7).

Did you ever wonder what that woman would have done if she lived in the desert or on a mountainside with no friends or neighbors for miles away? As grandmothers — and as women of any age — we all need a little help from our friends from time to time.

When your "oil" is low, through loss or sorrow, friends can help you find your way back to the one who gives the "oil of joy instead of mourning" (Isaiah 61:3). If your doors of opportunity are stuck, friends can wield some "WD-40" encouragement and help you open other avenues (1 Thessalonians 5:11). And if your body "squeaks" through age or illness, they can add laughter to oil your spirit (Proverbs 17:22). If you're hurting financially, their jars are available in a pinch (2 Corinthians 8:5).

> *When we give what we have in love to another,*
> *God will multiply and use it to provide another's needs.*

Some of our friends' and neighbors' jars may be small, while others are huge. But it's not the amount they hold that counts, but their willingness to give what they have. In the widow's case, God allowed the neighbors to share in a miracle.

He will do the same for us. I would venture to say that when the widow's need diminished, she returned the borrowed jars of oil. The next time, a friend or neighbor could be knocking on *her* door — or ours. And that new supply of oil could be God's provision for someone else's jar.

As a grandmother, what "jars of oil" can you give away? Friendship, laughter, special skills, practical help, comfort, food, or even hugs? If money's the need, you may not even have a "widow's mite" to give. All you can contribute is another empty jar. But when we give what we have in love, God will multiply and use it to provide another's needs.

How many friends do you have? Don't ask for just a few. We need each other. With a little help from our friends, God may allow all of us to participate in his special, everyday miracles.

DAY-BREAK

Is your "jar" of oil running low? What are your special needs right now? How has God used others to help you at times? Ask God to help you meet new friends and make you a part of his miracles in another's life.

DAY-BRIEF

Good friends know how to give, ask — and receive.

DAY-VOTEDLY YOURS

Lord, thank you for friends and for what they mean in my life. Help me to share what I have, whenever you ask. It all belongs to you!

day 22

mentor-pause

These older women must train the younger women to love their husbands and their children, to live wisely and be pure.
Titus 2:4 – 5 (NLT)

Candy held out her hands in a mock act of surrender. Everywhere she looked, she saw chaos: the commode overflowed, her carpet littered with dump trucks, dolls, and broken crayons, her clothes stacked to the ceiling in the laundry room, beds unmade, and kids fussing. She glanced at the clock. *And it's time for me to start dinner.*

Those are not the only situations that can describe a mother's day. Women of all ages — both stay-at-home moms and women with careers outside their home — struggle with life's daily challenges, from parenting, to marriage, to personal and spiritual growth. That's where your "grandmother-age" experience can help.

"That's up to their moms," you argue. And that's true, except that some women have long-distance moms. Others have lost their mothers, and some may have strained relationships with moms who can't emotionally or spiritually offer the help their daughters need.

Brenda Hunter says, "In an earlier era young girls grew up in the bosom of extended families with aunts, cousins, and grandmothers filling the role of mentors. They learned what they needed to know from women who naturally populated their lives."[2] Without those mentors now, women miss the rich blessing that age and wisdom can pass along to them.

Perhaps you're one of those grandmothers who run on a fast track yourself. When would you mentor someone else? "And after all," you say, "what can I possibly offer?"

A mentor is simply someone who shares her life with another, one who will come alongside, wrap her arms around them, and encourage them to keep on going. Whether you bring professional skills to the table, or simply serve coffee at your kitchen table, if you can lend an ear, or offer a hug and a prayer, God can use you to mentor others.

What women need and want to know, particularly young wives and mothers, is someone to help them answer questions like "How do I keep from killing my kids?" Or "Can I leave my husband for forgetting my birthday?" Seriously — and yes, I *was* just kidding — younger moms want to know how to survive the turbulent, child-rearing years and how to love their husbands when they're acting like bears. They want to pick your brain about being a wife, a mom, and a chauffer; and how to juggle a sixty-hour work week, how to tap into God's power, how to manage their homes, and how to stretch an already thin budget.

> *Through the everyday, plain events of your life, watch for women who need your life skills and wisdom.*

All God wants is your availability. Through the everyday, plain events of your life, watch for women who need your life skills and wisdom. Do you bake pies? Can you organize a closet? (Come to my house!) Know how to plan a great party? Complete a job résumé? Some women would love to learn your skills. Are you a mom? Grandmom? You can share from both your successes and your failures. Sometimes God builds our best ministries from our greatest weaknesses.

Have you lost a child? A spouse? Another woman with a similar experience may need to hear how you put one foot in front of the other, how you faced every morning, alone. How did you survive so many years and could still step into the rain smiling?

Through the years God has brought younger women to my doorstep. But he's also brought older women to my kitchen table. Sometimes being the "older" mentor may mean you, younger in age, are only a step ahead spiritually. But your wisdom is still needed. You may even be thinking, "Hmm. I could use a mentor myself right now."

Brenda Hunter says, "Mentoring, particularly in midlife, prepares us for an emotionally rich old age."[3] She says the sharing of our wisdom and experience will help shape our society as well. It will take all of our efforts: moms, grandmoms, mentors, and more — to influence our nation with godly wisdom.

Mentoring women may take different forms: from one-on-one sharing to small group teaching, from lunch sessions to internet counseling. But I find it does even more for me than prepare me for that rich, old age. Surprisingly, in many ways, it actually extends that age by making me feel years younger. Think of it as — mentor-pause.

Regardless of who's mentoring whom, it's a plan God set in motion long ago. It worked then, and it still works today.

DAY-BREAK

Have you ever mentored another woman, or has someone mentored you? What was that experience like? Think about young women you know who might need a strong, godly influence in their lives. Talk to God about being a mentor to someone, and ask him to show you what you can share from your life's experiences and skills.

DAY-BRIEF

Mentoring is simply sharing the footprints of God in our lives with someone else.

DAY-VOTEDLY YOURS

Lord, thank you for the beautiful privilege of mentoring others. Use me, Lord, and whatever skills or experiences I can offer. Help me to make a difference for you.

everyone's granny

Her children arise and call her blessed.
Proverbs 31:28

She's not even a grandmother; yet she's everyone's granny. Ruth Inman had no grandchildren by her own kids, so she "adopted" her friends' children and grandchildren through the years. In fact, she and her husband followed some of those dear friends to East Texas years later. Ruth ended up living on a county road outside of town dedicated almost entirely to one whole family — and their grown kids and grandkids. So she "adopted" them as her kids as well.

"The neighborhood children are nearly grown now, but together we shared ice cream and tears on many an occasion — and they still drop by for ice cream," said Ruth.

Soon after moving to Texas and that neighborhood, one of the adult sons there started introducing her to everyone as "Granny Ruth." Apparently the name stuck. "Even years later," she said, "when I meet people for the first time and I introduce myself as 'Granny Ruth,' many say, 'Oh, *you're* Granny Ruth!'" Ruth said it's much like a stone in the water. Her name has that sort of rippling effect that precedes her.

I think I know why. But I probed a little more into Ruth's past. She has served God in numerous ways through her life. Playing the piano and acting as secretary for a mission church as a young wife, teaching a Sunday school class for seventh and eighth grade girls, as well as leading a women's class, working in Vacation Bible School in her church, and serving on mission and staff search committees — these are just a few examples. She's both a fixture and a lifesaver for her adult choir — as a singer and as one who keeps the music and members organized.

But Ruth's middle name could be called "Encourager," and that's probably one of the main reasons she's everyone's "Granny." God tendered Ruth's heart for young teen girls and boys early on, and she has looked for ways to connect with them and encourage them with cards and notes. When she observed one of the youth in our church taking a younger, unruly child under his wing during her Vacation Bible School class, Ruth did some wing-tucking of her own — and helped blossom that youth. When another teen lost his father, Ruth sent cards and has expressed concern constantly.

When her daughter came to Ruth heartbroken because of her inability to bear children, Ruth encouraged her gently with words from Isaiah 54: "Sing, barren woman, you who never bore a child; burst into song, shout for joy, you who were never in labor ... For your Maker is your husband — the LORD Almighty is his name" (Isaiah 54:1, 5).

Successful "grand" mothering has more to do with how many "children" you've nurtured in the Lord rather than with how many descendants adorn your family tree.

Ruth has adopted scores of other families and their kids in various places, and they still connect, exchanging pictures, notes, and even occasional visits. If you asked people in our church and community how many of them had ever received an encouraging word or card from Granny Ruth, the number would be staggering — whether they're eight years old or eighty. She happens to be one of five women who pray for my family and me, and for my speaking and writing ministry — and the cards I personally have received from her would fill a huge box alone. And the thing is, when Granny Ruth says she's praying for you, you know she is.

No one thinks of Granny Ruth as a "senior." She looks like she just stepped out of a fashion magazine; and you only notice the few crinkles (not wrinkles) around her eyes because of the tears that glisten when her tender heart shines through.

Perhaps Ruth understands the deeper meaning of successful "grand" mothering. It has more to do with how many children you've nurtured in the Lord rather than with how many descendants adorn your family tree. Like the woman in Proverbs 31, Ruth "speaks with wisdom, and faithful instruction is on her tongue." No one could ever say she eats the "bread of idleness" (and in hospitality, she is queen) (vv. 26 – 27). Ruth, of course, would be quick to point out her flaws — but her "grandchildren" hardly notice.

Married almost fifty-nine years, she is a mentor, a role model, and an ageless grandmother to scores of children, youth — and adults. I have a feeling that one day in heaven someone will ask her if she has any grandchildren. And before Granny Ruth can smile and answer, a throng of children will arise — and call her blessed.

DAY-BREAK

Have you ever "adopted" others as your grandchildren? Ask God to show you how you can be an encourager and a grandmother to many who need God's touch on their lives.

DAY-BRIEF

Wrinkles come from miles of smiles.

DAY-VOTEDLY YOURS

Lord, help me to see the needs of others around me through your eyes. Give me words of encouragement and wisdom to share with those who need a touch from you.

day 24
freedom behind bars

The important thing is that in every way, whether from false motives or true, Christ is preached. And because of this I rejoice.
Philippians 1:18

Taura (Mrs. T, as the students called her) pulled the bed covers up a little closer to her chin and sighed. How she missed teaching! She loved her students, who were like grandchildren to her. A serious infection had invaded her body following a simple outpatient procedure. Now she faced months of recuperation. In many ways she felt imprisoned by her illness.

A younger teacher took over her class, and she obviously had differing ideas about teaching than Taura. She ridiculed Taura's former methods as being old-fashioned and allowed the children freedoms that bordered on disrespect.

When some of the children dropped by to visit Mrs. T and told her about the new teacher, at first Taura was hurt. The children repeated rumors that the new teacher was out to get Mrs. T's job. But instead of lashing out against the teacher, Taura encouraged the students to respect her and to follow their new teacher's directions. "You can learn from anyone," she said, "if you have the right attitude. Just remember who you are and why you are in school."

After the kids left, God reminded Taura of her own words to

the children. So she started praying for the students, naming them one by one as she had done before. This time she added her teacher replacement to her prayer list. She wrote notes to the younger teacher, encouraging her, letting her know she was praying for her. The teacher ignored the notes and refused to respond. Still Taura prayed. And as she did, God filled her with a new joy and peace.

Someone else faced a similar situation as Taura. The apostle Paul found himself in a Roman prison with nothing but time on his hands. With the powerful preacher now behind bars, others boldly stepped up to take his place. Rumors flew around faster than the Roman guards could draw their swords, and Paul heard the latest from faithful friends who visited him.

Apparently, not every preacher's motives were exactly on the up and up. Some, envious of Paul's popularity, tried to outreach and outreach his scope of influence. They wanted a name for themselves. Others had purer motives. Evidently, his followers expressed concern about these young upstarts trying to replace Paul.

But few things ruffled Paul's feathers, and he responded, "No matter what their motives, Christ is being preached. That's what counts!" Furthermore, he added, "because of my chains, even more good things are happening. It's actually helped build confidence in the Lord and caused believers to share the gospel more boldly" (Philippians 1:14, author's paraphrase).

We can channel our voices, our actions, and our prayers — where they can do the most good.

News that might cause another prisoner to rage and plot revenge only filled Paul with a continual joy (Philippians 1:12 – 18). Paul remembered who he was — a servant of Christ — and what he was here for: "For to me, to live is Christ" (Philippians 1:21). And Paul's letters from prison to his friends and "students" probably influenced them more than all of Paul's sermons put together. In a sense, we, who have benefited from those biblical letters of encouragement, are like Paul's grandchildren — way down the family tree.

No doubt Mrs. T's "adopted grandkids" in school, and even her own grandchildren, learned a powerful lesson outside of class. At times, revenge may appear sweet. We can rage or we can stew. We can retaliate or sue. Or we can channel our voices, our actions, and our prayers — where they can do the most good. To say we need divine help is an understatement.

But the important thing is not who's trying to hurt us or even why. We grandmothers know that by now. The lesson to learn — and to share — is that we help model Christ's love and message to everyone, no matter what.

It's a truth that will break through any prison.

DAY-BREAK

How do you handle unfair criticism or hateful actions aimed against you? What will you do this week to model Christ's love? Who will you add to your prayer list?

DAY-BRIEF

Actions aimed at "getting back" often backfire at you.

DAY-VOTEDLY YOURS

Jesus, when I'm tempted to retaliate, remind me of who I am and what I'm here for. May your love overcome any thoughts of revenge in my heart.

faithful love,
faithful example

*I am reminded of your sincere faith, which first lived
in your grandmother Lois and in your mother Eunice and,
I am persuaded, now lives in you also.*
2 Timothy 1:5

Evree awoke in the early morning hours from his fitful sleep and wiped his clammy hands on the sheets. *The dream, again.* He closed his eyes, willing the images to reappear on the screen of his imagination. *What does it mean? How will I find out? Who can tell me?*

At the breakfast table, Evree pushed his fork in circles around his plate of steaming, hot cereal. Thoughts of his troubling dream lingered. *Father will not understand. I'll ask Mother later.*

"Aren't you hungry, Evree?" his mother inquired. Father looked up, but said nothing.

"I have a headache," he hedged. "May I go lie down for a few minutes?"

After Evree's father left for work, his mother went to her son's room to check on him.

Before she opened her mouth, Evree poured out his story. "Mother, I cannot hold it in any longer. I have been dreaming of Jesus. I know it is he. And he is telling me to come to him. What does it mean? I cannot tell Father. He does not believe. He will not understand. And I am afraid to say anything to him."

"We will talk to your grandmother tomorrow. She will have wise words to offer." Evree's grandmother, a woman who knew God for many years, had first told Evree about Jesus. Evree's mother felt confident that the grandmom could counsel him.

Some of you can identify with Evree's grandmother or another grandmother named Lois. Both your circumstances and hers may differ from the above fictional scenario, but you know what it's like to have an unbelieving son or daughter or daughter-in-law/son-in-law. You've prayed faithfully and shed tears for them and your grandchildren for years. Your child and grandchild may know Jesus, and God has given you opportunities on many occasions to counsel them.

Grandmother Lois may not have been wealthy, but she was rich in faith. Her grandson, Timothy, grew up in a divided home. Lois, his Jewish mother, stayed faithful to her Greek husband. But he remained a stranger to her faith. Grandmother Eunice taught her daughter well and continued to influence her grandson, Timothy. No doubt, because of that heritage, he met the apostle Paul one day. That meeting resulted later in Paul's taking Timothy as his "disciple." Timothy later ended up as pastor of the church in Ephesus.

Never give up loving, hoping, teaching, and praying for your grandchildren — and your own children — that they will awake from their "sleep" to embrace Jesus, their only hope.

It's happening all over the world today. Young people respond to the gospel message of Christ, but anti-Christian beliefs in the home may bring division. For many, their very lives are on the line. To confess Christ brings instant death or abandonment.

While that happens less in America, families still deal with the conflict of differing worldviews. Faith can unify families, but it can also divide them. In Timothy's case, there's no indication that his father interfered. But because his grandmother is mentioned by name, we see a snapshot of her strong role in Timothy's life.

Whether your children and grandchildren deal with those issues or not, you, as a grandmother, can make a difference in their lives. You may live close enough to take them to church or to special children's activities, or even to teach them yourselves. We are seeing more and more grandmothers step into that role in our own "generational" church situation — even where families have lived in the same town for decades. Sometimes a grandmother is the sole Christian influence and the only stabilizing force in a child's life when they're being torn apart by divorce or unconcerned parents.

If the unbelieving parent is your own child, you may not understand what went wrong. Your faith didn't "take" with them. And now you feel your greatest mission is to help instill those values and ideals Christ taught to your grandchildren.

Just remember that faith is not an "inoculation" you can inject into your grandchildren that will protect them from every ungodly "disease" that comes along. Your efforts may seem fruitless at times. But never give up loving, hoping, teaching, and praying for your grandchildren — and your own children — that they will "awake" from their sleep to embrace Jesus, their only hope.

Let God give you guidance. He is omniscient; he knows his plans for your loved ones. He is faithful; he will not abandon them. He is El-Roi, the God who sees; and his ears are always open to your prayers.

Someday, someone on your family tree, or a member of your "family tree of faith," may say of your faithful grandchild: "I am reminded of your sincere faith, which first lived in your grandmother."

Those are the words all of us grandmothers long to hear.

DAY-BREAK

Do any of your grown children live in a household of "divided faith"? How has God given you "Grandmother Lois" opportunities to share in your grandchildren's spiritual heritage? Pray for your grandchildren this week. Send them a note with your favorite Bible verse in it and tell them how much you love them.

DAY-BRIEF

Your grandchildren can't inherit your faith, but they can "adopt" it.

DAY-VOTEDLY YOURS

Lord, I pray for my grandchildren, that they will choose Jesus above all other loves. Help them to be strong, no matter what divisions they may encounter.

day 26
preparing the place

My Father's house has plenty of room; if that were not so, would I
have told you that I am going there to prepare a place for you?
John 14:2

The news that changed my title from "mother" to "grandmother" transformed our home as well. We started filling up the empty spaces in the garage with secondhand and garage sale treasures: baby bed, infant swing, children's books, and toys — lots of toys. I wondered if people thought we were expecting one of those "miracle" babies — at our age — or if they were used to giddy first-time grandparents preparing for their first grandchild's arrival.

I also pawed through old boxes from our attic containing some of our own children's used playthings, still in good shape. Then I sanitized everything with some disinfectant wipes and soap and water, and stored them away for our grandchild's first visit. Of course, tiny fingers and minds couldn't wrap themselves around some of the toys or books we bought — not for a few months or even years. No matter. We were having fun, preparing a special place for them.

When another grandchild joined our family tree and the first one outgrew the pack 'n' play, the house seemed to shrink. One bedroom housed my home office. That left one bedroom besides our own, for guests. Unfortunately, it wouldn't hold a baby bed and a guest bed too. So we added a room. No, not as in *building* an actual room. We enclosed the dining room with doors at either entrance. Through the years it has become the baby room/play-room/dining room/library. We knew the kids would only use it a few times each year. But we wanted them to know we had created a special place just for them.

I eventually bought large tubs and divided up the growing stash of toys, storing age-appropriate ones in each box to match each grandchild's interests. Each time before their visits, my husband and I begin our grandparent ritual: setting up the mobile sleeping quarters and hauling in the colorful tubs.

I know I'm not alone. Others, like my friend Linda Silman, whose grandchildren only live twenty minutes away, love to "prepare the place" for their grandkids. Linda stores all of the kids' crayons, toys, and books in one closet and has a special playroom they can call their own. A few years ago, she and her husband even saved up and put in a swimming pool and a cabana where their grandkids can gather with other friends. Inside the house, they often spread pallets on the floor where the kids watch movies or even entertain the adults with their fun dramas and skits.

Both my mother-in-law and my own mother inspired me to prepare a special treat for each child either before their visit or when we travel to visit them. Both grandmothers were generous to a fault. I still remember my own girls' question as soon as their grandmother walked through the door: "Grandmommy, did you bring us any s'prises?"

*Every child, teen, and even adult likes to know that they have
a permanent, prepared place in someone's heart.*

Preparing the place for our grandchildren doesn't require great
expense. Before our grandkids arrive or when we travel to see them,
I buy gift bags to hold their "s'prises." The gifts are usually inex-
pensive dollar items, but the kids don't care. I keep a special treats
jar just for them near the kitchen, and a craft box in one closet,
stuffed full of paints, paper, fabric, and interesting textures for art
projects. Before one visit, I sent a special email invitation: "You're
invited to 'Mimi's Crafts'" and then listed the date and time.

Why are those things important? Because when we take the
time to do special things for others, whether for our friends, neighbors, kids, or grandkids, we are saying to them, "You are important to me. I'm thinking about you. You're worth the effort." Every
child, teen, and even adult likes to know that they have a permanent, prepared place in someone's heart.

It's something Jesus modeled to his own disciples. Just before
his death he tried to comfort them and prepare them for the coming events. Their hearts and minds still couldn't wrap around Jesus'
words, but one day they would understand. He let them know of
their value to him and to his heavenly Father.

Soon Jesus would be leaving them and joining his Father
again, back "home." There, Jesus would spend time preparing a
wonderful place for them to come — and visit? No, he's preparing a permanent place, adding whatever is necessary and making
their rooms special so they can live where he is someday. The most
beautiful part about Jesus' preparations is that they include those

of us who know Jesus as well. We too have a permanent place in his heart and home. We're that important to him!

Preparing the place for your grandchildren (and for others) is just one way we can let them know how important they are and that they will always have a "place" in our hearts.

DAY-BREAK

How have you prepared the place for your grandchildren (and others) through the years? What will you do this week to let them know they have a special, permanent place in your heart?

DAY-BRIEF

We always have a permanent place in God's heart.

DAY-VOTEDLY YOURS

Jesus, thank you for the place you are preparing for me someday. I can't wait to see the s'prises you have waiting there. Most of all, I'm looking forward to seeing you! Help me to make my heart and home a special place for others too, especially for my grandchildren.

day 27
a matter of rights

In your relationships with one another,
have the same attitude of mind Christ Jesus had.
Philippians 2:5

"I've earned the right to feel this way."

"I can do what I want."

"Who cares, anyway?"

"Doesn't age give me some privileges?"

"I'm not responsible to anyone but me!"

You may have heard those words flying out of other grand-mothers' mouths, or you may have said — or thought — them yourselves. As a nation we embrace "rights" like children hug teddy bears. Trying to persuade emotions otherwise can bring, um, major resistance. And grandmothers can clutch them as tightly as anyone.

Don't we have a right to our opinions, our actions, our possessions, and our lifestyles? The majority of us have lived at least five decades — long enough to gather some clout and wisdom. After all, we *do* know a thing or two. Don't we?

But knowledge and wisdom don't necessarily mean the same thing. Knowing something and acting wisely can shake out as opposite as night and day. When it comes to rights, we often leave wisdom out in the dark, clinging instead to our own preferences and patterns.

True wisdom marches to the tune of a different drummer. It's that upside-down theology that Jesus taught that leaves us a little mystified. "The wisdom that comes from heaven is first of all pure; then peace-loving, considerate, submissive, full of mercy and good fruit, impartial and sincere" (James 3:17).

It's the kind of wisdom Jesus exemplified throughout his life and ministry. He knew something about rights. God designed the plan for his Son to leave heaven and bear the sin weight of the entire world. Jesus, "being in very nature God," could have argued, "No! I have a *right* to my authority. I will give it up for no one. Why should I set aside my crown?"

But Jesus was "full of mercy," "peace-loving," "submissive," and "sincere." He cared more about us than he did about his rights. He refused to take selfish advantage of his role. Instead, he "made himself nothing" by becoming like a servant. Still totally divine, he humbled himself and became totally human.

Why would Jesus do that? Because he knew that his death was the only way to give us the supreme "right" to a full life on earth, the "right" to enter heaven, and the "right" to become his children. Jesus loved us more than he loved life (Philippians 1:6 – 11; cf. John 1:12; 3:16).

> **It's impossible to cling to our own selfish rights while yielding ourselves to God.**

As your grandchildren watch you interact with others and as long as they are young, they may acknowledge you're one smart cookie. Grandmothers know everything then! But as kids grow older, does that "smartness" — that knowledge — they observed in you translate into loving, practical wisdom? Do they see a sweet humility — or a resistance to change? Are you modeling a me-first attitude — or a generous, peace-loving nature? It's impossible to cling to our own selfish rights while yielding ourselves to God.

Your grandchildren are not the only ones who will be affected by your attitudes. In reality, we all have accountability to each other as members of the body of Christ, no matter how many years we've lived. That's both a privilege and a protection.

Oswald Chamber says, "Whenever our *right* becomes the guiding factor of our lives, it dulls our spiritual insight."[4] Is it easy to give up those rights? No. Is it our nature to put others first? No, unless we respond from our new, wise nature — the "same attitude of mind" Jesus gives us when we choose to follow him. Jesus knows our weaknesses, but he loves us in spite of them. He is always there to help us, reminding us that wisdom doesn't necessarily come from age. It comes from him.

Remember, as you release your rights to God, he will exchange them for something far better. Any "rights" he gives us then become privileges. Even your older grandchildren may see the change and boast about you: "Grandmothers are so wise!"

DAY-BREAK

How long has it been since you had an attitude adjustment? What "rights" do you struggle with the most? Will you release them to Jesus today?

DAY-BRIEF

When Jesus flashes a "yield" sign, he has a good reason.

DAY-VOTEDLY YOURS

Jesus, how I want your mind and attitude to rule my life! Fill me today with wisdom that is peace-loving, sincere, and full of mercy. I submit my rights to you, Lord.

day 28

i remember grandma

The memory of the righteous will be a blessing.
Proverbs 10:7 (NIV)

There's a special gift called memories God has given to each of us. No two are the same. Gratefully, we record those celebrations and bring out each one, carefully boxed, whenever the heart needs a smile or a sweet reflection, such as a snapshot of a loved one, journeys at home and afar — warm thoughts we cherish and remember. And though some may have lifestyles that are generations apart from their loved ones, no thoughts encourage us more than reminiscing about our grandmothers.

Mildred Henderson Watkins loved people. She was generous, kind, and thoughtful of others' feelings, especially children. When she and Grandpa would take neighboring kids to church, they always carried shoe polish so that she could polish the children's shoes on the way to town. Shiny shoes may not have mended a tear in a dress or a missing button on a shirt, but it brought a smile to the kids' faces as they entered the church building.

Grandmother Mildred never made it past the eighth grade. But as she and Grandpa rode to the fields to check on irrigation water, she would often read aloud to her grandkids from a huge volume of poems, stories, and essays. Her granddaughter Millie Daniel, named after her grandmother, says she often begged Grandma to let her read from "the book" too.

In spite of being a gardener, a farmer's wife, a mother of seven, and a "grandmother" to all who knew her, Grandma Mildred took care of her pretty hands. She enjoyed "dressing up," and polishing her nails was especially fun. Millie said, "Grandma had a wonderful saying my girls and I still repeat today. Placing her hands with newly painted nails up to her cheeks and feigning surprise or alarm, she would bat her eyes and announce, 'Have you seen my cows?' Of course her intent was to have you notice her lovely hands. It has become a catch phrase of ours to get others to notice our newest 'lovely thing.'"

Mama Kate Walls, Martha Brook's grandmother, was a woman of large stature — big-boned and tall. She had one arm much larger than the other. Due to breast cancer the year Martha was born, Mama's lymph nodes had been removed from that arm, making it swell often. But that never seemed to slow her down.

Mama Kate had an extra large heart. She loved God and her family — in that order. That's what mattered to her in life. Martha said her grandmother taught her about God, love, and moral fortitude and how to be a southern young lady. She helped her see the importance of reaching out to others, no matter what the need. Mama Kate even taught Martha patiently how to cook and sew.

These blessings — these portraits of our loved ones — are the fabric of our inheritance.

Mama disciplined when necessary. But she was also the kind of grandmother who worried about you at age sixteen if you didn't wear your "undershirt" when it was 70 degrees outside. Martha was eighteen when she lost her grandmother in a second bout with cancer. "Forty years later," says Martha, "I still miss her."

Sometimes our memories run deeper as we rehearse the powerful, life-changing ways our grandmothers influenced us. What does Amy Huelskamp remember most about her Grandma Phyllis? "She took me in for two years when my mom was getting her 'life' together, and she taught me about being organized." From her, Amy learned practical skills like housework, yard work, and making chocolate chip cookies. She taught her how to be independent and how to save money, and she prepared her for future life decisions.

Amy says one memory especially brings her comfort. She had chicken pox and wanted to call her mom badly. They couldn't reach her, however, so Amy's grandma served her hot chocolate and cookies and tried to soften her misery by helping her identify with Jesus' pain on earth. She said to remember that pain on earth is only temporary and that it helps us look forward to heaven, where there's no more sickness or pain. And then Grandma sang hymns to her.

Years later, Grandma Phyllis died, unfortunately before Amy could say goodbye. Amy's husband left too. Her family lives far away, but Amy knows she is not alone. Grandma Phyllis taught her she could truly depend on God for everything.

Life calls us back to schedules, school, work — or wherever

God plants our feet. And once again, we pack up our boxes of memories and set them back on the shelf. But they are never forgotten. These blessings — these portraits of our loved ones — are the fabric of our inheritance.

Blessed indeed is the one who can celebrate the memory of a godly grandmother.

DAY-BREAK

What memories can you share about your grandmother? Take time today to celebrate those memories with your own children and grandchildren. If your remembrances don't bring celebration, focus on making your own relationship with your grandchildren one that will give them reason to celebrate their memories of you.

DAY-BRIEF

Our memories may fade, but heaven never forgets.

DAY-VOTEDLY YOURS

Lord, thank you for the precious memories of my own grandmothers. Show me how to make new memories with my grandchildren, each time we share life together.

day 29
the great adventure

May you live to see your children's children.
Psalm 128:6

When a woman reaches "grandmotherhood," does she suddenly abort the spirit of adventure? Perhaps some do, but not Patricia Lorenz's grandma. Here's her story:

"Even though my grandmother, Emma Schwamberger Kobbeman, died when I was pregnant with my second child in 1970, she has become one of my all-time favorite role models. The memories I have of her spirited nature helped me survive some rough times during my struggling years as a single parent of four children.

"Grandma Kobbeman's husband died during the Great Depression in 1932 when she was just forty-two years old. Her five children were twenty-three, twenty-one, twenty, nineteen, and twelve. From that day on, she struggled with poverty, single parenting, and trying to find work with only a fourth-grade education. But she never lost her sense of humor or her spirit of adventure.

"By 1960 Emma was a grandma with twenty-four grandchildren, all who lived close to her home in the Sterling Rock Falls area of northern Illinois. During the late 40s, 50s and early 60s, we'd gather for huge family picnics in Sterling's Sinissippi Park not far from her home. This beautiful park along the shores of the Rock River was filled with Indian lore, including a number of Indian burial grounds on a bluff overlooking the river.

"As Grandma Kobbeman's five children, their spouses, and her two dozen grandchildren arrived on picnic days, carrying enough food for Chief Black Hawk's entire army, we spread out among the tall pine trees to enjoy time together.

"I remember one picnic especially well. It was the time Grandma Kobbeman decided to ride the go-cart. Perhaps she ate too many sweets that day, or maybe it was the sight of her entire, immediate family gathered in one place that made her feel especially frivolous. Whatever it was, we held our breath when Grandma made the announcement that she was going to ride the go-cart by herself. With her hands on her hips and a twinkle in her eye, she walked straight over to the go-cart and announced in a loud clear voice to her oldest grandson, 'Larry, show me how to run this thing.'

"The go-cart belonged to cousin Larry, who had built it from scratch. The body looked rough, but the engine was a piece of mechanical art that Mario Andretti would have been proud of. When Grandma Kobbeman plopped her ample backside down onto the wooden seat and then stepped on the accelerator with her heavy brown oxfords, that little engine threw itself into World Cup competition.

"As we cousins watched from a distance because she'd outrun us in the first ten seconds, Grandma whizzed past three dozen giant pine trees, then flew across the make-shift track Larry used to test his wonder machine. Within a few seconds she sailed right into the baseball field.

"She would have made a home run except she missed second base by fifty feet. She barely missed the popcorn stand, however, and then headed straight for a forested area that led directly to the river.

"With both arms flailing in panic, Grandma's heavy oxfords pressed even harder into the accelerator. She yelled, 'Stop this thing! How do I get it to stop?' As she headed for a row of poplars, narrowly missing two oversized oak trees, she must have experienced total body panic.

"Both of her legs shot out in front of her as she released them from their death-grip on the accelerator. She quickly came to an abrupt halt in front of the sacred Indian mounds at the edge of the water. Chief Black Hawk, the favorite son of Sinissippi Park, would have been proud of her.

"Needless to say, Grandma spent the next two hours telling and retelling the story of her go-cart adventure to all the relatives and even some strangers who happened by.

"From horse carts to go-carts, Grandma displayed a keen sense of humor, an unbridled spirit of adventure and a deep faith in God that I treasure as part of my heritage.

"Thanks to Grandma's sense of adventure, I have raised four spirited children of my own as a single parent. Since becoming a single grandmother myself, I've ridden an alpine slide down a steep mountain; braved a motorcycle ride on a busy California highway, clinging to my daughter's waist; snorkeled off the coasts of a dozen islands; took a sunrise flight in a hot-air balloon over the Arizona desert; and traveled alone for two days on two planes and two busses to Kuala Lumpur, Malaysia, to attend the wedding of a woman I'd only met once."[5]

> *The things you're willing to try with your grandkids*
> *may move you out of your comfort zone,*
> *but they will also land you smack in the middle*
> *of your grandkids' hearts.*

That's great for grandmothers like Patricia, but what if you don't feel … adventurous? After all, you do hope to *live* to see all your children's children. Stephen and Janet Bly say, "There's great comfort in routine … But good grandparents muster the strength and courage to plunge into new activities. There's no retirement from grandparenting."[6]

Perhaps all grandmothers like a certain amount of predictability in their lives. But your grandkids would probably love to see a spirited side of you too — especially if it involves them. Grandparenting *is* an adventure, and one that God highly recommends. The things you're willing to try with your grandkids may move you out of your comfort zone, but they will also land you smack in the middle of your grandkids' hearts.

That makes any "adventure" well worth the risk.

DAY-BREAK

What kinds of adventure have you tried with your grandkids?

How has God used your own mother or grandmother to strengthen your faith? Make a list of adventurous activities you're willing to try soon, alone and with your grandkids.

DAY-BRIEF

With God, every day is a great adventure.

DAY-VOTEDLY YOURS

God, thank you for so many examples of men and women who chose to make life an adventure with you. Help me involve my grandchildren in some great experiences designed especially for them.

day 30
a grandmother's tears

You keep track of all my sorrows.
You have collected all my tears in your bottle.
You have recorded each one in your book.

Psalm 56:8 (NLT)

Grandmothers know how to shed tears. After all, they were first mothers. And what mom hasn't wrung her hands in worry and cried tears like Niagara Falls for the welfare of her children?

Sometimes the tears spring up because of joy and answered prayer. Kim True tells how fear and worry overcame her the day her daughter called to say she was pregnant. Because of health issues, she took medications that put her baby at a high risk for fetal abnormalities and death. Yet not taking those same medications raised the risk for her. Kim sought the help of godly people who prayed faithfully for her daughter and unborn child and left the results with God, determining to give him praise regardless of the answer.

Kim says, "I can't describe the tears and emotion we felt as we looked at the first sonogram and saw a perfect little spine, normal arms, legs, and counted the fingers and toes of our first grandchild."

At other times our emotions as grandmothers may catch us off guard, especially when the outcome turns out different than what we had hoped. Jeanne Dennis felt the sting of hot tears from her heart when she heard the news about her daughter's pregnancy crisis, involving her first grandchild. "Our daughter went into labor four and a half months early. The next morning, she called and tearfully told me that her baby had been born alive but died within a few minutes. Her grief was understandably intense, but I was not prepared for my own grief.

"Watching my daughter and son-in-law go through such excruciating emotional pain and feeling the loss of my grandchild so keenly led me into a three-month battle with depression ... My season of hope had turned into a season of loss."

Jeanne had just written about the need for total trust in God. She said, "When my first grandchild died, I had to live out what I had written. When we go through the deepest valleys, somehow we have to believe that God knows what He's doing, and when the pain feels overwhelming, we can climb onto our heavenly Daddy's lap and cry. And He'll cry with us."[7]

Sometimes our grandkids' tender hearts bring a rush of tears to our eyes as well. My aunt Ramona said when her husband died, her five-year-old granddaughter ran up to her, threw her arms around her neck, and cried, "Come live with us, because you will be so alone."

Another time when Ramona was keeping her grandkids for the weekend, her seven-year-old grandson woke up from a bad dream, crying. Ramona comforted him, as grandmothers do, by telling him Jesus was watching over him and would be with him all the time. He finally drifted off to sleep.

The next morning Ramona asked him if he was feeling better. His little three-old-sister heard them talking and asked him what had happened, so he told her about his dream the night before. She asked him if he cried. He said yes. She replied, "Why didn't you wake me up? I would have cried with you."

We stayed with our granddaughter a few days when our daughter had her second baby. The first night after Caden's birth, while Jen was still in the hospital, I started tucking my granddaughter into bed for the evening. As soon as the covers reached her face, her chin started quivering, and she began tearing up. "I miss my mommy and daddy!" she sobbed.

"Why don't we call Mommy and Daddy and tell them good night?" I suggested.

No one understands our tears like Jesus.

So we did. But afterwards she was still crying. So I crawled in bed with her and started singing songs to her about Jesus that I had sung on many nights with my own children during tearful times — and some of the same songs my daughters had both repeated to their kids. After a few moments, she calmed down, and I kissed her goodnight.

Tears can have a powerful way of bringing our relationships closer, including our intimacy with God, whether in times of extreme loss, discomfort, or anxiety. Grandmothers agonize and empathize with their children over tragedies involving their grand-children; they intercede tearfully with powerful prayers over rebel-lious loved ones or when families split, and they cry when injustice, violence, or ridicule affects their children or grandkids' lives.

But no one understands our tears like Jesus. To him, every teardrop, like a snowflake, is unique in its own way. And the One who bottles all our griefs, the One who has experienced true sor-row himself, records every tear that falls. Sometimes gushing like a fountain or at other times flowing gently like a stream, each tear begs to share its story. But as the teardrops glisten in the light of the Son and fall from each grieving heart, the Father adds his sweetness — until they form a liquid fragrance as costly as the most expensive perfume.

One day, God will not only wipe away every tear from our eyes. Perhaps he will also present to us the very bottle of tears he has kept as a treasure near his heart, so that we can pour it upon his feet — our sacrificial offering of praise to him.

DAY-BREAK

What tears have you shed as a grandmother? When have your grandchildren's tears brought emotion to the surface for you? This week, pray earnestly for your grandchildren, especially for any dif-ficult situations they may be going through.

DAY-BRIEF

Tears cleanse the heart and help us see heaven a little clearer.

DAY-VOTEDLY YOURS

Jesus, thank you for bottling all my tears and for understanding my foolish grandmother fears. Keep my grandchildren near your heart, where I know they will remain safe.

day 31
gifts from the heart

They have scattered abroad their gifts …
their righteousness endures forever.
Psalm 112:9

The widows gathered around the upper room holding up their hand-made garments and mourning the death of their beloved friend Dorcas. A woman known for doing good and helping the poor, Dorcas touched many throughout the community with her unselfish time and gifts.

When some disciples heard that Peter was nearby, they sent for him. The apostle came and prayed for Dorcas, and God raised her from the dead. The news spread, and many came to know the good news of Jesus because of what happened to her. God was not finished with Dorcas — or her gifts (Acts 9:36 – 42).

God continues to bless even the simplest gifts from grandmothers, in the lives of those who knew them. Cynthia Kramer remembers the small but special gifts her Czech grandmother of nine boys presented to her grandkids each time they left her house after a Sunday visit: a sack of candy with their names on it. On birthdays, Albina gave each a personalized birthday card with nickels taped all over it — a huge gift to small fries then.

Susan Barringer says her granny gave Susan's children the gift

130

of time. "Grandmother" changed to "Nanny" when her newly widowed granny moved into their basement to care for Susan's three small children. "Because my husband and I both worked outside the home, Granny played dolls and dress-up, and threw tea parties with her granddaughters. She even made time to go fishing in the creek with her grandson."

"Granny is now ninety-five, living with my mom, and spends most of her days sitting in a chair blankly staring, her hands moving in a sewing motion," says Susan. "Sometimes, on rare occasions when I visit her, Granny remembers me. On one such moment, I took her hand in mine, leaned down close to her, and asked, 'Granny, what will you be when you grow up?'"

"She smiled sweetly and replied, 'I'll still be your granny.'"

Susan said she hugged her, they both cried, and then her granny was "gone" again. But she recognized that God had given her a gift that day, one that she will always cherish.

Like Dorcas, Penny MacPherson's grandma constantly looked for ways to bring happiness to everyone. Penny says, "Grandma was always working on homemade outfits for them, and she sewed many a wedding dress — including one for me. No one left without something to wear if Grandma could help it."

During the holidays, her grandma would wrap for days — often losing track of some presents because there were so many. "Sometimes," says Penny, "you'd have to go back for another meal to retrieve the stashed gift. But that was a blessing because Grandma had a beautiful way of making everyone feel welcome and as if they belonged there."

For Kim Coffman's grandmother, Estelle Smith Songer, money was scarce but love wasn't, especially at Christmas time. Kim says, "I can't remember ever getting a store-bought gift from my grandparents. But I can recall a ten-foot-tall Christmas tree (or so it seemed), sparkling with tinsel and piled high with gifts that Grandma had spent countless hours crafting or sewing through the year. With nine granddaughters and limited resources, home-made was all she could afford. She gave us crocheted purses, linen sets for our dolls, decoupage plaques, stuffed animals, and (as we grew older) quilts and pillowcases for our 'hope chests.'

"One year, after a long struggle with a heart condition, Grandma died a week before Thanksgiving. The upcoming holiday season seemed somewhat empty, and we did our best at Thanksgiving to remain cheery. I felt thankful that Grandma's struggles were over. I knew she now lived in the presence of Jesus. But hollowness prevailed in our togetherness, and I found myself dreading Christmas even more.

"As the season approached, the traditional Christmas preparations kept us busy and our minds preoccupied. Eventually, Christmas morning without Grandma arrived. The lighted tree sparkled and the wonderful aroma of my mom's fantastic cooking hung in the air, as my sisters and I gathered at our parents' house. Watching my own kids enjoy Christmas filled me with a new sense of expectancy. I felt a little like a kid again myself.

"When no more gifts appeared under the tree, we assumed that was all. But then my mother pulled out three more — one for me and for each of my sisters. The writing on the tags confused us a little: 'From Grandma.'

"'What's this?' we asked.

**God will resurrect the kindness shown,
the gifts given, the good deeds, and the godly
influence of each one to live on.**

"'Go ahead and open them,' my mother gently encouraged us.
I slowly tore away the paper. Inside each package we found kitchen
towels, gifts made by my grandmother's loving hands earlier in the
year — now passed on to us by my mother's loving hands.

"Tears blurred my vision as my older sister openly wept and
my younger sister wiped at her eyes. Mama just smiled. 'I knew
she would want you girls to have these,' she said. And I know that
Grandma was smiling too."[8]

At her grandmother's home, Danna Appleby said her family each took a turn opening all their Christmas gifts in a special
chair — like kings and queens — starting from the youngest grandchild and working their way up to Grandmother Mauldin. As the
family grew, their time to open gifts grew longer too, and the little
ones could hardly wait for their turn in that place of honor. "It's
such a delightful tradition," says Danna, "that my cousins, siblings,
and I still continue it in our own homes."

Most of our grandmothers have already passed from this life,
and so will we. But like Dorcas's life and the lives of these special
grandmas, God will resurrect the kindness shown, the gifts given,
the good deeds, and the godly influence of each one to live on — as
our stories are told from one generation to the next.

Grandmothers can make a difference.

DAY-BREAK

What gifts from your grandmothers influenced you most? What kind of "heart gifts" do you give your own grandchildren? Take time to write down how you would most like to influence your grandchildren.

DAY-BRIEF

Gifts from the heart are the ones we never forget.

DAY-VOTEDLY YOURS

Father, show me how to make a difference in the lives of my own grandchildren. And thank you for so many grandmothers who have paved the way before us with their examples of godly love.

day 32
the best kind of medicine

A cheerful heart is good medicine.
Proverbs 17:22

Kids hate taking medicine. Didn't you, as a child? I mean, some of those concoctions were gross! Remember those weird antics we tried just to get our kids to open their mouths and say "Aaah," so we could fly the "airplane," that dreaded spoonful of medicine, into its "hangar" (their mouths)? We knew our kids would feel better once they took what the doctor ordered. But convincing them to do it? That's another story!

God knew there would be times in grandmothers' lives when they needed just the right medicine. So he prescribed grandkids. Almost without fail, their fun, quirky comments lift our spirits and bring instant smiles to our faces — and sometimes downright healing to our bones!

Dr. Edna Ellison's only grandchild lives four hundred miles away, so her granddaughter "hugs and kisses" her through the phone. On one visit to her granddaughter, Edna heard her comment to her little friend: "Your Mimi is square," glancing from her friend's grandmother back to Edna, "and my Mimi is round."[9]

Brenda Sampson's two-and-a-half-year-old granddaughter calls her "Sassy." But it's a toss-up as to which one of the two wears that title. One day her granddaughter wanted to go outside and kept saying, "Let's go outside — okay?"

Brenda told her it was too cold to go outside. Her granddaughter simply replied, "Sassy, get a jacket, and you will be *all right!*"

Gracie Malone has experienced her share of laughter from her grandchildren through the years. She shared this about her granddaughter Abby: "Shortly after her fifth birthday, I pulled her onto my lap, kissed her on her forehead, and said, 'Abby, I remember when you were born. I was there. You were the cutest little thing —'

"At this point, she interrupted boisterously by exclaiming, 'I know, I know! I was in my mom's tummy trying to get out and my mom was puuushhhing and puuushhhing.' Abby let out a huge grunt, 'Aaaaarrrrrrggghhhhh!' With wild hand gestures and an animated tone, she continued. 'Then I gave her two big karate chops — *Yahhh, Yahhh* — and out I came.' She brushed out a wrinkle in her skirt, grinned, and added, '*Ta-dah!*'"[10]

> *God knew there would be times in grandmothers' lives*
> *when they needed just the right medicine.*
> *So he prescribed grandkids.*

Karen-Atkins Milton, one of Elden Kyle's grandmothers, said her grandson walked in and saw her sitting in her chair after one of her major surgeries. "He came running and jumped into my arms to hug me. Well, his daddy nearly had a heart attack and told Elden Kyle to 'Be careful and don't *hurt* Meems!'

"So I thought it would be a good idea to show four-year-old Elden Kyle my incisions so he would better understand why he couldn't jump on me (big mistake). Needless to say, the sight of those huge, criss-cross stitches scared him. He made a 'claw' with his hand and said, 'Did a monster scratch you?'

" 'No,' I said, seriously. 'The doctor did it.'

"To which Elden Kyle whispered this response to his daddy: 'That doctor needs a spankin'!' "

Recent studies by cardiologists at the University of Maryland Medical Center indicate that laughter may prevent heart disease and even lower blood pressure.[11] Laughter is great medicine!

Apparently hospitals, nursing homes, and other groups are hiring professional "laugh leaders" to accelerate healing, an idea actually influenced by an Indian guru.[12] The professionals could have saved themselves some money. God designed laughter long before anyone started measuring its effects, and Solomon wrote about it in the Bible.

If children truly laugh four hundred times a day, compared to adults with their fifteen giggles, then the solution for a healthier body is obvious to us grandmothers.[13] *Just spend more time with your grandchildren.*

DAY-BREAK

Record some of the funny things your grandchildren say and place them on the refrigerator or mirror. Keep a notebook of fun, clean humor to share with your older grandkids. If nothing else, try laughing out loud for ten minutes. You'll feel better.

DAY-BRIEF

A laugh a day keeps the heart at play.

DAY-VOTEDLY YOURS

Lord, thank you for the happy sounds of children's laughter. Teach me to laugh more and stress less.

day 33

down on her knees

For the LORD is good and his love endures forever; his faithfulness
continues through all generations.
Psalm 100:5

Some grandmothers never live long enough to know how their prayers and their lives truly influence their grandchildren. Does God hear their cries? Does he answer? Do our prayers make a difference? Michelle and Kris can both share a hearty, "Yes!"

Michelle Frazier, a mom of two boys, recalls the prayers of her granny, Efna Ann Burton: "This night was like many others spent with my grandparents in their white box-frame home in the small Texas town where I grew up. A windy, cold night set in as the first winter front blew through on the end of a day that had reached the mid-seventies. By nightfall it was in the upper thirties, and Granny headed for the quilt box.

"The homemade quilt box was as wide as a full-sized bed, just as tall and deep, made of stained wood by Granddad, a mechanic/farmer by trade, a carpenter when necessary. I watched as Granny's hands reached in and brought out cotton sheets, two worn blankets, and two quilts. The quilts were made of squares of familiar colors and patterns. They brought warm thoughts just looking at them.

"I crawled upon the antique bed, quickly curling my body beneath the sheets. At night the heaters were turned way down or not on at all. Granny's hands pulled up blankets, then quilts, tucking me in tight, the weight of them bringing to mind the phrase 'snug as a bug in a rug.' After I prayed my childlike prayer, she turned out the light and left the room.

"Time passed and they themselves readied for bed. Granny peeked in on me, and I played possum. She left the door open just a bit, and went to her own bedside. In the shadows I saw her kneel down and the effort it took for her to do so. In quietness surrounded by the winds I listened to Granny talk with her Lord, her God and her Savior. And I learned what it meant to intercede, to cry out to the Lord, to listen, and to give thanks.

"I felt guilty for eavesdropping on Granny. But I have come to believe God intended for me to hear those prayers. And I know over the years I have received the blessings from those priceless prayers uttered by my precious grandmother."

> *God's faithfulness connects with the prayers and influence of godly grandmothers, and we — and those to come — are blessed as a result.*

Kris Brown remembers the powerful influence of her grandmother too — especially her prayers. She says, "Easter vacation was always a highlight of the year when I was growing up in booming southern California. I cherished the thought of spending a week in Tarzana, without my siblings, on a calm, San Fernando Valley farm.

"Grandma always awakened me at four or five a.m. and asked me to sit in a chair and listen while Grandma and Grandpa read the Bible, devotionals, and prayed (at length). Grandma would then fix breakfast before Grandpa left to work. After devotions, she sent me back to the bedroom to sleep — or at least to stay in bed until 8:00 a.m.

"It wasn't until Grandma Peterson died in 1985 that I realized the profound foundational heritage that she had instilled in me spiritually. She engraved a desire on my heart to learn God's Word and pray, one that influenced me to receive my college degree in Bible.

"But seeing Grandma live out Jesus in her daily life impacted me the most. I never knew the Pauline that was born in White Russia. Her family escaped the czar on foot and fled to Germany. I never knew the person, who, according to other relatives, smoked like a chimney, drank like a sailor, and developed quite a vocabulary for a lady in those years. I only remember the Grandma whose life drastically changed at the first Billy Graham Crusade in Los Angeles in 1949. I treasure the God-fearing and people-loving woman who cherished God's Word with devotion and consistency.

"Grandma Peterson gently put God's thumbprint on every area of my life. Even in college and as a young married adult, I knew that Grandma was praying for me every day. Now that I am a grandmother, I zealously 'march' on my knees in prayer on behalf of my own granddaughters, Landry and Audrey."

Only heaven knows how our own mothers and grandmothers' prayers — and lives — have influenced us. We know that our ancestors' ungodly tendencies and patterns follow us even to our own grandchildren (Deuteronomy 5:9–10). And God always gives us a choice and an opportunity to break that chain. But what a comfort to know that God's faithfulness connects with the prayers and influence of godly grandmothers, and we — and those to come — are blessed as a result.

What a faithful God we serve!

DAY-BREAK

What do you remember about your grandmother? How did she influence you the most?

DAY-BRIEF

Prayer reaches corners nothing else can touch.

DAY-VOTEDLY YOURS

God, thank you for your faithfulness to all generations — especially to mine. You have blessed me in so many ways through the influence of my grandparents. May those who come behind me see the tracks of your faithfulness clearly.

day 34
sufficient grace

*My grace is sufficient for you, for my power is made perfect
in weakness ... That is why, for Christ's sake, I delight in weaknesses
... in difficulties. For when I am weak, then I am strong.*
2 Corinthians 12:9 – 10

Karen Atkins-Milton, now age fifty-four, was once a hard-driving,
working mom. "I had everything going my way until about six or
seven years ago," says Karen. "Then everything changed."

"I was just a shy girl from Muleshoe, Texas, but my parents
taught me a strong work ethic. I took *so* much pride in being the
first to arrive at work, the last to leave, and the best at whatever I
did. That kind of effort put me in a position of vice president and
CFO of a prominent engineering firm in Dallas, at the young age
of thirty-three. I eventually rose to a professional height of senior
marketing professional and an associate of one of the largest engineering firms in the United States.

"In the beginning of my career, I taught myself needed skills.
Yet I knew God had designed those natural abilities. I loved my
work so much that I would have done it for free if possible. I
tried to serve God faithfully, sharing my faith when God led. I
commuted over an hour, using that time to pray and learn music
tracks. I left before 6:00 a.m. so I could talk to God before work

as I sat in the parking lot. I didn't return home until 7:00 or 8:00 p.m.

"I had always *said* my priorities were God, family, and work — in that order — but inevitably I faced the truth: I was a workaholic! At one point in my life I surrendered to full-time Christian service in a music-related capacity, but the doors never opened to pursue this. In reality, God knew that I would never quit work on my own. I thought our family's existence depended on my continuing to work. I was *so* wrong. I knew my pride wouldn't let me quit, either.

"At the peak of my career, I developed back trouble. I tried to ignore it by taking pain medicine. Eventually, the pain grew intolerable. For years, doctors misdiagnosed my true condition, because they focused on a more painful area in my shoulders and arms. I had eight shoulder surgeries before doctors correctly identified my condition as degenerative disc disease. That's when the spine surgeries began — and my career faded.

"Something new or unusual resulted after each surgery. The first fusion failed and was repeated. Another surgery on my cervical spine left the screw accidentally poking into my spinal column, which had to be corrected with yet another surgery. Lumbar surgery went bad. That led to a blood transfusion and more surgery. After eight spinal surgeries — sixteen operations in six years — I began seeing the writing on the wall. I couldn't work anymore. Basically, my career ended early with disability.

"It seemed as if my life was over, as depression and loneliness set in for almost two years. I didn't feel sorry for myself; I just felt that I could no longer use the talents God had given me. It was as if God had catapulted me to the top, then plunged me to the bottom, like an amusement park ride out of control. I was scared, and I couldn't see any silver linings. Medicines (including steroids) for pain management caused major weight gain, swelling, more depression, and numerous debilitating side effects.

"The only things that sustained me were the support of my husband and family, the prayers of my church family — my friends in the body of Christ — and my own personal relationship with Jesus that had begun when I was young.

"A turning point in my life came last summer when my mother fell and broke her pelvis. God used that to put me on the road to physical *and* emotional recovery. I knew God had orchestrated my being there at the time she fell. I felt so blessed that I wasn't working, so I could help her — just like she had helped me through all my lifetime of surgeries. God restored physical stamina to me that I thought I had lost forever. When Mom needed me, God miraculously raised me up and gave me strength through my weakness. In fact, he did more miracles than I have room to tell."

Even in our weakest moments,
God will make us strong, if we depend on him.

But God didn't stop there, Karen said. "I eventually increased my walking from one time around the block to 'prayerwalking' three miles a day, with prolonged times afterward in God's Word. I lost weight. Relationships grew as God gave new energy — and more time — to spend one-on-one with friends, children, and grandchildren. When I worked, I had prided myself on my self-sufficiency, but now I depend on Christ more than ever.

"During those draining times, I also learned to depend on my husband. His support — emotionally, physically, and spiritually — helped me so much, and our relationship has grown deeper. I joined hand bells in my church, and as I sing solos, the words and music mean even more now than before. My husband and I also continue to lead a Bible study and worship time at one of our local nursing homes."

Does Karen still deal with pain? Absolutely. Some days, she says it's worse than others. Depending on the weather, it can be excruciating, especially since she's chosen to endure more of the pain rather than chance the side effects of being overmedicated again. Now that she's a "stay-at-home wife and grandmother," Karen sees scores of things to do — things she's always excused with "I could do that — if I didn't work." She does her best, but even simple tasks often make her body cry, "Enough."

In spite of her weakness, Karen says, "God has taught me so much since disability forced me to leave work. I've learned that as long as I am here on this earth, God has his own 'work' for me to do. Most of all, I know that in my weakness, he is my strength."

Some of you can identify with Karen. Whether you deal with physical pain or other disabling circumstances, you know what it's like to face the same battles daily. Sometimes we can't wrap up life in pretty packages with colorful bows. But even in our weakest moments, God will make us strong, if we truly depend on him.

God's grace is sufficient for Karen — and for all of us grand-mothers too.

DAY-BREAK

How have you felt the fear of weakness and loss of independence in your life? How has God restored praise to your lips? If you are in the middle of a debilitating depression, take time today to reaffirm your dependence on God.

DAY-BRIEF

Praise is the perfume left when a child of God has been crushed.

DAY-VOTEDLY YOURS

God, when I am weak, your strength shows up best. I can do nothing by myself. Today, I'm declaring my dependence on you.

grandma's growing green

The righteous will flourish like a palm tree ...
They will still bear fruit in old age,
they will stay fresh and green.

Psalm 92:12, 14

"No, Me-Ma, don't touch that!" cried six-year-old Caitlan. "Here, let me show you how to do that."

Jettie's daughter Karen had given her a computer years ago when Me-Ma Jettie was in her seventies. Caitlan, one of Me-ma's granddaughters, coached her grandmother through some of her early sessions as she was trying to learn how to use that computer. Me-Ma Jettie felt "green," to say the least.

What a contrast to the teaching methods Jettie used and the skills she taught during World War II! Only a junior in college at the time, Jettie received special permission for a few months to teach shorthand, bookkeeping, and typing at the local high school because of the shortage of teachers.

But Me-Ma Jettie caught on to technology quickly. "All my grandkids have helped me with learning computer skills: Caitlan, Tracy, Robin, and Jeffrey. They set me up an email account and taught me what *not* to do. They even loaded games on the computer and taught me how to play them. Now I email my kids and grandkids often. I've also stayed connected through email with other family members, a special missionary couple in Africa, and a single teacher in Germany."

Jettie also learned how to use a cell phone, but her loved ones get aggravated if she doesn't carry it with her.

Jettie's children and grandchildren live miles away, but that's what makes her newfound technology so helpful. "My grandchildren keep up with me, like calling me to pray for one of their tests," she says. "Our special relationship started when they were little. They would write me letters, sometimes asking me to cook their favorite dishes." One granddaughter is now a pharmacist, who helped her during her husband's illness.

Jettie, now a great-great-grandmother, is not afraid to learn. "Dial-up" has caused its share of frustrations for Me-Ma Jettie, so her grandson is helping her switch to cable. And she's adding a web cam to her computer so she can "see" her grandkids through video chat.

She only lacked a year and a half of college when she returned home during the war. "I've thought about finishing my degree lots of times," Jettie said.

"You still can," I challenged her. "You might be able to complete your degree online." And knowing this eighty-something grandmother's spunk and willingness to learn, I wouldn't be surprised if she did.

Iris Wilson contacted me and told me how texting was strengthening her relationship with her grandchildren. When she requested a Christmas list from her thirteen "grands" last year, one of the granddaughters wrote "devotional book" at the top of her list. Iris supervised my book table at a women's retreat where

I spoke one year, and she returned home with two copies of my devotional journals, *Daily in Your Presence*, based on the names and attributes of God.

Iris said, "Rachel and I decided to read and journal each day from these books and then talk about some of the things that we learned. About two months later she asked me to 'text' a Scripture every day to her, so in the back of the book I post the one I send. In 3 John 1:4 it says, 'I have no greater joy than to hear that my children are walking in the Truth.' I can now add knowing that our 'grands' are also walking in the Truth."

One evening Iris texted her college grandchild to ask a question, knowing college kids keep late hours. After a great conversation, her granddaughter sent this message: "Grandmother, you are sooooooo cool! I don't know of any other grandmother who texts her 'grands'!"

Some older grandmas may plead, "I feel like a dinosaur when it comes to new technology." True, what's easy for one person may be extremely difficult for another.

But some refuse to change, insisting that "the old ways" are just fine, thank you. We can find many ways to "flourish" and to "stay fresh and green" in our old age, but why not use every means possible to connect with precious loved ones, especially those who live far away?

Your willingness to try says volumes
about your desire to keep growing and about your
attempt to understand their world.

It's okay to share about your world growing up. But a blend of the old and new is good for both your grandchildren and you. Grandmother Iris says between email, texting, and IMing (instant messaging), she can be a part of her grandchildren's lives, even though they live so far away. You don't have to join social networking sites to build a relationship with your grandkids, though you might find this statistic interesting: women over age fifty-five make up only 3 percent of the current 7.5 million Facebook contributors, but in a three-month period, they grew faster than any other group — by 175.3 percent. (Just remember, *some* kids might be embarrassed if Grandma "friends" them on Facebook.)[14] Do what fits you — and your grandchildren.

If you need help, ask your grandchildren to teach you. God often works through the mouths of "babes" — and the process of learning together may strengthen your bond as much as anything — as well as broaden your world to reach others.

Bearing fruit in old age has more to do with your character and God's faithfulness than your technological abilities, so don't stress. Fear motivates many who refuse to learn or change: *What if I fail?* But what if you succeed? Your willingness to at least try says volumes about your desire to keep growing and about your attempt to understand your grandkids' world. One day your grandchildren might entertain the thought of "giving up," when school tests or life dilemmas challenge them beyond their capacity to understand.

Hopefully, our attitudes in life to keep green, growing, and going will inspire them to say, "If Grandma could do it, so can I!"

DAY-BREAK

How do you use modern technology to help strengthen your grandchildren relationships? List one new skill you would like to learn, and plan how you will use it with your grandkids. How can you inspire your grandchildren to keep growing in character too?

DAY-BRIEF

Admitting fear or ignorance is often the first step toward success.

DAY-VOTEDLY YOURS

Lord, show me every way possible to connect with my grand-children, so I might keep on growing — and bearing fruit for you, even in my old age.

day 36
on the run again

Be still, and know that I am God.
Psalm 46:10

"Hi, Hon! I sure miss you and the kids! Are you planning to visit anytime soon?"

"Hey, Mom! We were just talking about wanting to get together. It's crazy here. Work, church, kids' school schedules, you know how that goes. We have one weekend open this month, the twenty-fifth. How about if we come then?"

"No, I have a conference that weekend. What about the next month?"

"Um ... yeah, the twelfth. We could come then."

"Whoops. Actually, between my schedule and your father's, every weekend is booked."

Some of you have had that conversation with your kids — numerous times, especially if they live miles away. Today's boomer-grams are constantly on the run. Unlike their grandmas, modern grandmothers may slow down only long enough to get their 500-mile tune-up at the doctor's office, before picking up speed again. Some of their calendars show fewer blank spaces than their own children.

And the activity doesn't stop with boomer-grams. Because seniors are living longer — and working harder — many older grandmas fill their days with ceaseless activity as well. Just check out a church's senior adult ministry schedule. Their energy sometimes both inspires me — and tires me. And I am a boomer-gram myself.

So how does that affect your relationships with your kids and grandkids? That depends on you. But what can you do to change your life and out-of-control schedule?

Remember that God gives each of us choices — and the same number of hours in each day, every week, month, and year. We can say, "Yes" or "No." Are those choices easy? Not usually. No matter how hard you want to keep your priorities right, life often slips in to rearrange them, like a thief who switches price tags on store merchandise without your awareness.

Someone once said, "One realizes the importance of time only when there is little of it left."[15] Do you remember how time flew with your own children? You thought you'd defy nature and spend mega-moments with your kids. One day they were watching *Sesame Street*. Then it seemed like the next day you turned around, and they were grown and buying houses of their own. Moms don't get "do-overs." But neither do grandmothers.

> *We come to know God and his plan for us as we quiet our hearts and listen — really listen.*

Make a special effort to be still and slow down. Some of you already work at the second part of that. But do you get "still"? (I know, some of you "run" so hard that you start snoring the minute your body and mind grow still.) Yes, God speaks to us while we're on the run. But more times than not, we come to know God and his plan for us as we quiet our hearts and listen — really listen.

One-size-fits-all won't work here. What God whispers personally to you may differ from his words to this grandmother's heart — as to how you find solutions. We all go through challenging seasons. And some of you are still working forty-plus hours a week in high-maintenance careers. But the overall principles in God's Word stay the same. Life is too short to miss God's best. And his best is never running through life, waving to the ones we love as we pass by.

Whatever you can do to make more time for precious relationships, do it. Don't just count time, watching it fly away. Knowing he is God and that he will answer you is the first step in making time count for you and those you love.

DAY-BREAK

How often do you sit still, just to "know that he is God"? Is there anything in your life and schedule that needs rearranging so you can spend more time with those you love?

DAY-BRIEF

Saying no to lesser important things helps us say yes to the best things.

DAY-VOTEDLY YOURS

God, you know me so well. I give you my life and my schedule as a blank page. Write on it the things that matter most. I want to know you — and the ones you give to me — much better.

a reason for hope

Always be prepared to give an answer to everyone
who asks you to give the reason for the hope that you have.
But do this with gentleness and respect.
1 Peter 3:15

I overheard them talking from several rows back on the plane. I glanced back to see an older woman and a young international about nineteen or twenty years old, engaged in a serious conversation. They talked nonstop for almost the entire two-hour flight.

The grandmother spoke with excitement and joy, answering the young man as he questioned her in broken English. I overheard bits and pieces: "hope," "trust in Christ," "plan for you," "joy," "heaven," and I smiled with understanding. The woman was intently sharing her faith in Jesus. Just before the plane landed, I heard her ask the young man, "Would you like to pray with me?"

After we stepped off the plane, I found the woman and told her how glad I was that she had a chance to share about Jesus with the young man. "He is a new believer in Christ!" she grinned.

On another occasion I was attending a conference several hundred miles away. A cab driver in the taxi in which I was riding started a conversation. He was a follower of Christ, and had driven a taxi for thirty-two years. "I always wanted to take more music and play the saxophone, but friends told me I couldn't play jazz and be a Christian."

I encouraged him to follow his dream again, that it was never too late to accomplish what he might have been — or what God might want to do through his life.

"I'm living proof of that," I said, before exiting the taxi.

Some women think by the time they're grandmothers they have more limitations and therefore, fewer opportunities to live out and share their faith in Christ. Not so. In my own church, senior women have helped serve both the physical and spiritual needs of the homeless in places like Dallas and New Orleans. Many have given "life" away both in their apartment complexes and in other countries around the world. For those who are retired or who have flexible schedules, the senior years are wonderful times to volunteer in places and with organizations that truly make a difference.

On a mission trip to Peru a few years ago, God gave me several opportunities to share my faith with those of various ages: children, young adults, and grandmothers like myself — on the streets, in their homes, and in Vacation Bible Schools.

Each time I shared my testimony, a young Hispanic man interpreted for me. I had watched in amazement as this same young man led one after another to Jesus on a bus — in the amount of time it would take me to brush my teeth. On one particular occasion, we talked to a grandmother and daughter on the street. The grandmother, in tears, nodded in agreement when I asked if she would like to know Jesus personally. As we were finishing our conversation, the young adult daughter interrupted. The interpreter explained to me what she was saying. She had wanted to trust Jesus from the very beginning of our conversation, but we misunderstood her desire. Before we left, both said yes to following Jesus.

When I saw the interpreter again at our reporting time back in the States, he apologized to me. "All those times I was interpreting your story, I was using a word that means 'cloth' in Mexico, but 'fingernails' in Peru." (My testimony told how my pastor father had used a special liquid solution and cloth to explain God's love. That visual illustration influenced me greatly to follow Jesus at an early age.) I told the interpreter not to worry. The people understood God's love and message anyway.

> *There really is no right or wrong way to share*
> *the reason for the hope and joy inside our hearts*
> *— except to "do this with gentleness and respect."*

We may miss God's opportunities often. I have. But one thing I'm sure of. There really is no right or wrong way to share the reason for the hope and joy inside our hearts — except to "do this with gentleness and respect." We are not robots, dispensing canned information. God calls us as women to genuinely care, to be life-giving encouragers, and we can all share his good news filled with hope. If we know Jesus and trust him to open doors for us; if we make ourselves available to him and acknowledge that it is he, not us, who does the work; then God will use us wherever we go. He may take us next door or to the next state. He may send us to another country, to another grandmother, or to our own grandchild. God's Word — and his message of hope — is not limited by anything or anyone.

Live in such a way that gives others a reason to question you about the "hope that you have." Others need your words, your example, your encouragement, and your hope. Simply be ready — and God's Spirit will give you the words. He will pave the way.

DAY-BREAK

What opportunities has God given you to "share the reason for the hope that you have"? If you have misplaced that hope, whom can you talk to this week to help you rediscover it?

DAY-BRIEF

Lasting hope can only be found in Jesus.

DAY-VOTEDLY YOURS

Jesus, lead me to those who need hope, and ones who are searching for you. Thank you for filling my life with your hope and joy. Your good news is too wonderful for me to keep silent.

day 38

questions, questions,
who's got the answers?

Since my youth, God, you have taught me …
Even when I am old and gray,
  do not forsake me, my God,
till I declare your power to the next generation,
  your mighty acts to all who are to come.
Psalm 71:17 – 18

"How big is God?" "What does he look like?" "How can God really love everybody?" "Does God ever sleep?" If you're around your young grandchildren very often, questions like those may sound familiar. I still remember my own daughters' questions that always seemed to come during their bath time or bedtime: "Mommy, how will Jesus come back? Will he fly? Will he ride a camel?" Sometimes, they'd answer their own question: "I know …"

And children don't necessarily stop asking when they enter adolescence. Their questions only increase in intensity. "Why does God let bad things happen to good people?" "How come God didn't keep me from failing?" "How do I know there's really a God?" "Does God really care about my needs?"

As a grandparent, how would you answer those questions? You can pass the buck to your own kids, or you can reassure your grandchildren that you don't have all the answers. Only God does. Admitting you don't know is not a sign of weakness.

Sometimes that's an admission of wisdom. But teaching a child about God's character is one of the most important truths you can reinforce in your grandchildren's lives. God's Word is your sourcebook of wisdom for "declaring" his "power" and his "mighty acts to all who are to come."

Spend time anticipating the questions your grandchildren might ask ahead of time. Look up appropriate Scripture verses that will help them understand. Paraphrase them in your own words so you can give an age-appropriate response if questioned.

When you can't find a specific answer (and often you won't), focus on God's overall nature and simple truths in his Word: he is everywhere; he is love; he has a special plan for us; God hates sin, but not those who do bad things. As the grandkids grow older, they can grasp more. Praying together that God will teach you both will strengthen your bond together.

Share from your experience what God has taught you about himself. Sometimes, the questions our grandkids ask force us to go deeper into a study of God's character for ourselves. With wise guidance children will often answer their own queries in the process. One day my five-year-old grandson asked his mom, "So, what's life really all about?"

"Well, it's about loving Jesus, about knowing God and helping others know him. And it's about loving people — living out his plan for our lives," Val answered.

"And fun too, right?"

"Well, yes, Jesus says he wants to give us abundant life — one that's fun and full."

> *You may not have all the other answers.*
> *But you know the One who does.*

Jordan summed up the conversation with great authority, flexing his muscles. "And I know what it's full of: *power*, right?"

Sometime later, he was walking through a department store with his mom and the same conversation resumed. After a while, Jordan echoed his mother's final assessment: "Life's really all about Jesus, isn't it, Mom?"

Listening — as they figure things out — and sharing what you know with your grandkids is a privilege for grandmothers. Like moms, only in a supportive role, grandmothers too may have occasional opportunities for gentle guidance as our grandkids try to discover the answers to life's most important questions. Life really is all about Jesus. You may not have all the other answers. But you know the One who does.

That's what really counts.

DAY-BREAK

What kinds of questions have your grandkids asked you? How did you answer? This week, make a list of possible questions they might ask and of how you might answer. Start a personal study of your own about God and his character.

DAY-BRIEF

Jesus is the answer to all of life's toughest questions.

DAY-VOTEDLY YOURS

Father, teach me more about you. I confess my inability to understand life's hardest questions. But I do trust you, and I truly need your wisdom. Give me time to declare your great power and your faithful acts to all my grandchildren.

day 39
homesick

Blessed are those ... whose hearts are set on pilgrimage.
Psalm 84:5

No matter what age we're at, by the time we're grandmothers, we start thinking about the future a little more ... soberly. Yes, people are living longer, but our friends' faces start appearing in the obituary column. *They were so young,* we think. And the more birthdays we count off, the younger they seem. Death takes on a new perspective. Suddenly it's not something we will encounter one day. We could be peeking at heaven around the corner.

Questions like, "What have I done with my life?" "Have I accomplished all that God wanted me to do?" and "How long do I have left?" may cross our minds a little more often than before. Some grandmothers at this stage decide it's time to chase new dreams; others want to slow down and "smell the roses." Still other grandmas are already busy planning their own funeral service.

Younger grandmothers may not think about the fragility of life like those in their seventies or eighties. But none of us can deny the fact that our lives are constantly moving toward a climax. In reality, does it really matter how old we are? All it takes is losing one friend or loved one "prematurely" to understand the temporary nature of life. So what should our attitude be?

In Psalm 84, the writer reflects the feelings of a "pilgrim" in exile, longing for a return to "a place near your altar" (v. 3). Away from the one he loves, he describes the joy and desire for "home" — for living in God's presence again.

That's the same attitude God wants for us as we journey through life. We set our hearts on tangible things: homes, jobs, leisure — even people. Are those things wrong? Not in themselves. But if we attach ourselves too tightly to any of them, we lose our perspective and root ourselves in homes made of wood or brick. Those are the treasures we can touch and see and clutch in our search for security. But God wants us to hold them loosely in our hands.

Blessed — happy — is the grandmother who understands where home really is.

Blessed — happy — is the grandmother who understands where home really is. She knows that life's greatest treasures are not bought and sold. The simple things are what she celebrates daily and holds dear: the sparkle of friendship, the gift of love, the laughter of children, and the smile of God. She knows how fragile each day is and how precious and few are the things that really last.

After my mom was diagnosed with cancer with only a few weeks to live, I asked her if she was afraid to die. "No," she said. "I'm not afraid. I just don't know what it will be like."

Like most of us, no matter how much we study about heaven, we still come away with question marks. Those who know Jesus long for it, but they may wonder about that future home. Here's how I once summarized a few thoughts on heaven in a greeting card I wrote for Warner Press:

> There's no place like home, and there's no home like the one God is preparing for us someday. We cling to the familiar, not understanding that a far greater miracle awaits us when we cross from this life into eternity. There, Jesus waits to escort his own into a place of sweet peace and blessed rest. There, we can finally see with veil removed the beauty for which our souls have so longed to know. There, our loved ones wait with eager anticipation for us to celebrate with them the joys for which we were ultimately created. If we were allowed one glimpse of that place, our real home, we would not hold too tightly to the ones gone before us. Instead, we would grieve because we cannot go with them. Because home, after all, is where God is.

Maybe that's all we really need to know for now. Having our hearts set on pilgrimage means living in the awareness that any day could be our last day on earth and the first day of forever. It means that nothing in this world can compare to the joy one day of seeing our Creator, our Father, and our Savior face to face.

And it means every day we grow a little more homesick — for the place we'll one day call our real home.

DAY-BREAK

How do you feel about the future? Do you ever wonder what

heaven will be like? Is there anything you would have a hard time letting go?

DAY-BRIEF

Pilgrims know their destination — and the One who leads them.

DAY-VOTEDLY YOURS

Lord, the older I get, the more homesick I grow. Thank you for the promise of heaven, my real home. Thank you that you will be waiting there for me with open arms.

day 40

epitaph or legacy?

So the next generation would know them,
even the children yet to be born,
and they in turn would tell their children.
Then they would put their trust in God
and would not forget his deeds
but would keep his commands.

Psalm 78:6 – 7

There's something, um, "noble" about the thought of leaving a legacy. All grandmothers want to be remembered for something … worthy. Have you ever wondered what you'd like on your epitaph? Here are a few examples from history.

From a cemetery in England: "Here lies the body / Of Margaret Bent / She kicked up her heels / And away she went." A painter's tombstone reads, "A Finished Artist"; and a marker in Burlington, Vermont, says, "She lived with her husband for 50 years / And died in the confident hope of a better life." Another from Stowe, Vermont, reads, "I was somebody. / Who, is no business of yours."[16]

But that's not exactly how we want our lives summarized. In reality, you may have little say about the words on your grave marker, unless you sign an agreement with the company ahead of time. But your life says a lot about the kind of imprint you'll leave on your grandchildren's hearts.

A legacy is something we hand down and pass on from one generation to another. From the time your first grandchild enters your world, you are building the kind of legacy they will remember. The time you spend with them, God's love that you mirror, the kindness you show, the lessons you reinforce — these are the epitaphs they'll hide in their hearts forever.

Do your grandchildren really know you? Do they hear about your faith and godly devotion? Do they understand the passions of your heart? My mom was an accomplished pianist and up until her death, she could still scoot onto the piano bench and with long, nimble fingers play flawlessly those tunes and melodies by ear that she learned from her youth. We wanted to preserve her music for her grandkids and us, so my brother helped her record some of those songs onto a simple CD a short time before she died.

In addition, Mom took time years ago to type up the story of her youth for us. I kept asking her to write about her early adult life so we could pass that down to our grandchildren as well. While she lay in the hospital a few weeks before her death, we uncovered a cache of those stories in a pile of papers near her bed. Her grandchildren now read those treasured stories and discover things they never knew about their grandmother's faith. Her legacy lives on.

It's not what they remember
about the things we did that matters;
it's what our lives tell them about a faithful God.

But it's not just the tangible evidence that documents a grandmother's life in the hearts of those she loves. Sometimes it's the unseen, indescribable impressions of a giving heart in love with Jesus. Those of you who live close enough to invest hours and hours into your grandchildren's lives are fortunate indeed. Sometimes you may feel as if your grandkids know you ... too well. (Just remember, they usually do go home at night.) But they will remember your godly impact in their lives for years to come.

For the rest of you long-distance grandmoms, your legacy may depend on special moments and memories, things like we've talked about in this devotional. Your own legacy will mirror *your* God-given gifts, not those of others. Whether you hand down a journal of your thoughts, your prayers, a scrapbook of photo memories or favorite Scriptures, monetary gifts, or simple gifts of time, they spell memories with your name on it, written with love on the hearts of those who will benefit. Above all, pass down what God has taught you as he gives you opportunity.

Most likely you won't see short poems or cute phrases etched on today's gravestones. You'll probably see your name plus your birth date and "expiration" date, separated by a dash. Only those who knew you well can fill in the "dash."

But that dash represents a lifetime. What will your grandchildren think about you? In reality, it's not what they remember about the things we did that matters; it's what our lives tell them about a faithful God. A grandmother's deepest desire is that her descendants would ultimately "put their trust in God and would not forget his deeds but would keep his commands."

That's the kind of legacy we'd all love to leave.

DAY-BREAK

In a few sentences, write down what you most want your legacy to include. What are you handing down to your grandchildren?

DAY-BRIEF

The things that last are the things passed, from one generation to another.

DAY-VOTEDLY YOURS

Lord, of all the things I can pass on to my grandchildren, I want to leave a legacy of love — and a life that testifies to your faithfulness.

epilogue

Perhaps you have never come to know and enjoy the intimate presence of God personally. If he has placed such a desire in your heart, may I share with you some simple steps so you can become acquainted with him and become a child of God forever?

1. Admit the sin in your life and the need in your heart for God (see Romans 3:23).
2. Acknowledge that Jesus loves you and that he died for your sin (see John 3:16).
3. Recognize his salvation is a gift, not something earned (see Romans 6:23; Ephesians 2:8 – 9).
4. Ask Jesus to forgive you, to come into your life, and to fill you with his personal, intimate presence (John 1:12).
5. By faith, thank him that you are now God's child, and confess that from now on, he will be the Lord and Love of your life. Give Jesus the keys to all the rooms of your heart (see Romans 10:9 – 10).

If this book has encouraged you, I'd love to hear from you. And if I can help you in your Christian growth in any way, please let me know. For more information, see my websites: www.rebeccabarlowjordan.com or www.day-votions.com.

Rebecca Barlow Jordan

notes

1. Dennis Rainey, *Staying Close* (Nashville: Nelson, 2003), 273.
2. Brenda Hunter, *In the Company of Women* (Sisters, Ore.: Multnomah, 1994), 184.
3. Ibid., 187.
4. Oswald Chambers, *My Utmost for His Highest: An Updated Edition in Today's Language*, ed. James Reimann (Grand Rapids: Discovery House, 1992), May 25.
5. Patricia Lorenz, from "Go-Cart Grandma," first published in Oblates Magazine, 1984; used by permission.
6. Stephen and Janet Bly, *The Power of a Godly Grandparent* (Kansas City, Mo.: Beacon Hill Press, 2003), 22 – 23.
7. Jeanne Gowen Dennis, *Running Barefoot on Holy Ground: Childlike Intimacy with God* (Grand Rapids: Kregel, 2006), 106 – 7.
8. Used by permission of Kim Coffman (© 2009).
9. Used by permission of Edna Ellison (ednae9@aol.com) (© 2009).
10. Gracie Malone, *Off My Rocker* (Colorado Springs, Col.: NavPress, 2003), 27.
11. David Biello, "Laughter Proves Good Medicine for Heart": *Scientific American*; see www.sciam.com/article.cfm?id+laughter-proves-good-medi (accessed March 31, 2009).
12. Buck Wolf, "Laughter May Be the Best Medicine," *ABC News* (May 13, 2005); see abcnews.go.com/Health/PainMananagement/Story?id+711632&page=1(2) (accessed March 31, 2009).

13. Dan Johnston, "A Smile a Day Keeps the Doctor Away," www.articlebiz.com/article/a77-1-1smile-a-day-keeps-the-doctor-away (accessed April 3, 2009).

14. "Fastest Growing Demographic on Facebook: Women over 55" (February 2, 2009); www.insidefacebook.com/2009/02/02/fastest-growing-demographic-on-facebook-women-over-55 (accessed April 4, 2009).

15. E. C. McKenzie, *14,000 Quips and Quotes* (Grand Rapids: Baker, 1980; reprint: Peabody, Mass.: Hendrickson, 2000), 516.

16. "Epitaph or Legacy?" by June Shaputis, "Funny Stones to Tickle Your Funny Bones," at Web-panda.com: www.webpanda.com/ponder/epitaphs.htm (accessed April 8, 2009).

DAY-VOTIONS™
Rebecca Barlow Jordan

Day-votions™ for Grandmothers: Heart to Heart Encouragement

Day-votions™ for Women: Heart to Heart Encouragement

Day-votions™ for Mothers: Heart to Heart Encouragement

Introducing a new series of Day-votions™ from bestselling inspirational author Rebecca Barlow Jordan. This beautiful, lighthearted series of devotional books is perfect for you and is a perfect gift for women of all seasons, and all stages of life.

Available in stores and online!

Share Your Thoughts

With the Author: Your comments will be forwarded to the author when you send them to *zauthor@zondervan.com*.

With Zondervan: Submit your review of this book by writing to *zreview@zondervan.com*.

Free Online Resources at
www.zondervan.com

Zondervan AuthorTracker: Be notified whenever your favorite authors publish new books, go on tour, or post an update about what's happening in their lives at www.zondervan.com/authortracker.

Daily Bible Verses and Devotions: Enrich your life with daily Bible verses or devotions that help you start every morning focused on God. Visit www.zondervan.com/newsletters.

Free Email Publications: Sign up for newsletters on Christian living, academic resources, church ministry, fiction, children's resources, and more. Visit www.zondervan.com/newsletters.

Zondervan Bible Search: Find and compare Bible passages in a variety of translations at www.zondervanbiblesearch.com.

Other Benefits: Register yourself to receive online benefits like coupons and special offers, or to participate in research.

ZONDERVAN®

ZONDERVAN.com/
AUTHORTRACKER
follow your favorite authors